MW00999212

BOMBS AWAY!

The World War II Bombing Campaigns over Europe

John R. Bruning

ZENITH PRESS

For AlliLee:

No matter what happens, no matter who we become or where our lives take us, your unbridled heart and inspiration gave me the strength and passion to stay true to this journey.

First published in 2011 by Zenith Press, an imprint of MBI Publishing Company, 400 First Avenue North, Suite 300, Minneapolis, MN 55401 USA

Copyright © 2011 by John R. Bruning

All rights reserved. With the exception of quoting brief passages for the purposes of review, no part of this publication may be reproduced without prior written permission from the Publisher. The information in this book is true and complete to the best of our knowledge.

Zenith Press titles are also available at discounts in bulk quantity for industrial or sales-promotional use. For details write to Special Sales Manager at MBI Publishing Company, 400 First Avenue North, Suite 300, Minneapolis, MN 55401 USA.

To find out more about our books, join us online at www.zenithpress.com.

Library of Congress Cataloging-in-Publication Data

Bruning, John R.
Bombs away! : the World War II bombing campaigns over Europe / John R. Bruning.
   p. cm.
Includes bibliographical references and index.
ISBN 978-0-7603-3990-9 (hb w/ jkt)
1. World War, 1939-1945--Aerial operations. 2. World War, 1939-1945--Campaigns--Western Front. I. Title.
D785.B78 2011
940.54'42094--dc22
          2010042590

Maps by: Philip Schwartzberg, Meridian Mapping

All photographs are from official U.S. archives and author's collection unless noted otherwise.

On the cover: A Fifteenth Air Force B-24 drops its payload.

Printed in China

CONTENTS

While the British bombed at night, the USAAF remained committed to daylight attacks over Germany. Bomber Command switched to night raids after suffering heavy losses during the opening months of the war. The USAAF took huge losses at times, but solved that problem with the introduction of long-range escort fighters and drop tanks. Better protected from German interceptors, the USAAF ended the war with a lower loss rate than Bomber Command, despite operating throughout the war in daylight. Here, a group of curious RAF airmen receive a lecture from a USAAF officer on the Boeing B-17G Flying Fortress during an inter-service exchange late in the war.

Introduction

THE EMPTY SKY

SEVEN DECADES AGO, battles raged across Europe's flak-torn skies. That epic clash consumed tens of thousands of aircraft born from the factories of a dozen nations. Riding them down to their final, fiery resting places were men of passion, vision, and dedication. They died horribly, trapped in the machines that bore them aloft as flames engulfed them. Few deaths can ever reach that level of pain and misery.

Visit the battlefield at Verdun and the shell-torn land still harbors wounds even a century has not healed. Not so with the titanic struggle to control Europe's skies during the six years it took to defeat Nazi Germany. Those skies are empty now; there are no telltale scars to be found among the clouds. Time and the nature of the fighting have swept away every vestige of what will probably remain the largest air war in human history.

A few signposts of this clash remain here and there, off the beaten path ready for those who seek them out. An old Eighth Air Force bomber station, its runways now cracked and weed-riddled; local museums chocked with aircraft or memorabilia of an age that now exists only in fading memories of the final few who lived it—these fragments are all that is left. They cannot tell the total story of what occurred in the skies during those six years of World War II. It is just too massive, the forces engaged so large as to prevent most minds from grasping the enormity of the national commitments to such a new form of warfare. Instead, those museums and memorials, those airfields that once thundered with the sounds of hundreds of engines but have long since fallen into disuse, at best can provide mere hints of the magnitude of the struggle.

Some of those who fought in it survived to write their memoirs. Those are only tiny representative threads of a vast tapestry that ultimately claimed hundreds of thousands of lives, civilian and military.

It all started with a dream, a vision of how the next war could be fought without the stalemate of the Great War. The theorists posited, and the air crews put those ideas to practice with mixed results and a staggering casualty rate. Strategic bombing, the solution to static, attritional warfare, ultimately itself became a war of attrition and national resources. In trying to avoid more Sommes, more Verduns, the theories espoused before the war

The Allied strategic bombing campaign virtually destroyed Germany's urban centers. Hundreds of thousands of civilians died in the rubble and the firestorms created by the RAF's incendiary attacks. The morality and the effectiveness of such raids have sparked one of the most enduring controversies to emerge from World War II.

Home for the night. An exhausted Eighth Air Force crew brings a B-17 down on final approach over an airfield in East Anglia.

The incredible stress and psychological pressure repeated missions over Germany produced are more than evident on Tech. Sgt. Vernon Lindemayer's face in this photograph. Just back from another mission as a B-17's top turret, this image was snapped before he even had a chance to shave. Those who returned home after their tour in Europe did so as different men, branded forever by what their experiences in the air war.

created new versions of them in the sky. In the process, cities burned and civilians died right alongside the servicemen sent either to protect or destroy them. If Verdun consumed a generation of French, American, and German warrior sons, the inter-war solution of strategic bombing resulted in the mass destruction of Europe's most beautiful and culturally rich urban centers.

This book tells the story of that unique and exceptionally violent campaign through the photographs taken by noncombatants who rode into battle with the sole purpose of trying to capture these events for succeeding generations. Hundreds of these photographers died in the line of duty, killed when their bombers were shot out of the sky by flak or fighters. At war's end, tens of thousands of those photos were simply dumped on office floors in Eighth Air Force units all over East Anglia. Some of the men saw the value in those photos and scooped up some of these precious and historic images. They took them home as coveted treasures of the most difficult, and meaningful, time in their lives.

Most of those images never survived, and that is a significant tragedy given the level of sacrifice the photographers took to record them. The comparative few that do exist today survived an Air Force archive that bounced around among stateside offices, the Air and Space Museum, and finally the National Archives. In the process, they were stored improperly, and many have degraded to the point that they are no longer useful. America has never been past-centric; we have short memories. and the future is what matters to us as a people and a culture. In some respects, this is good. Some cultures cling so caustically to their histories that centuries-old wounds continue to affect their social dynamics. That is not the American way. We experience, then move on.

But here, within these pages, I would like to return you, gentle reader, to a time when thousands of aircraft darkened Europe's skies. It is a time when a generation of idealistic young men, steeped in the lore of flight through pulp magazines and movies like *Dawn Patrol* and *Hell's Angels* convinced them that glory awaited among the clouds. What they discovered instead was a thousand ways to die, a thousand terrors whose effects on the survivors of the campaign would last a lifetime, nestled in their nightmares and shared only with loving spouses—or at least the ones who stuck it out with them upon their return.

There was no help for them and PTSD (post-traumatic stress disorder) as there is now for America's warriors. They were simply expected to return home, pick up their old lives, and

Damaged bombers limping back to England often crash-landed and burst into flames. The USAAF developed the most sophisticated and well-equipped fire-fighting crews in the world to help save lives in such situations. Here, a team of fire fighters in asbestos suits hold chemical sprayers and await the call to action.

The bomber crews developed their own rituals and traditions, such as this one. When a crew member flew his final mission, he received a dunking upon return. It is a tradition that carries through in some U.S. aviation units to this day. Here Maj. Jim McPartlin gets the treatment in front of an Eighth Air Force B-17.

A 401st Bomb Group B-17G sits on an airfield in East Anglia after limping home with an engine afire after a mission in March 1944. As the fire crews sought to contain the flames, they burned through the top of the cowling. The engine's weight caused the cowl to snap and sag to the ground.

press on. But trauma and the human mind have an unpredictable relationship. The damage was done, and the effect of the air war on those who fought will linger until the final aviator from that long-lost age breathes his last. The war did not end in 1945; it simply changed form.

This book is an homage to these young men, those who died and those who returned hollow and spent by their combat experiences. The photos tell the story better than any words I will ever be able to put to paper, so they will take center stage on every page. Riding a B-24 to Berlin armed with nothing but a camera was no small feat of courage in 1944, but there were men who stepped forward and proved willing to do it. Their surviving work paints a vivid picture of the human experience that defined a generation of aviators.

In the myriad books written on the strategic bombing campaign, that human element seems all too often suborned to the technical aspects of the machines and weapons used to fight it. Book after book can be found with aircraft specifications: the number of .50-caliber machine guns in a B-17F or how to tell the difference between a B-24D, J, or M. There will be some of that in the pages that follow, but the focus will be on the men who flew the machines and the civilians on the ground who endured the fall of their bombs. Ultimately, history is not defined by how much horsepower a Wright Cyclone engine could produce; it is composed of human experience.

A few gallant writers—journalists and novelists whose patriotism drove them to England or Italy—rode into battle aboard these bombers in hopes of capturing that human experience. MacKinlay Kantor, a Civil War novelist, was one of those dedicated few who was rejected for military service due to his age. He found a way to serve his country and share his words with a nation eager to understand what its sons were doing in Europe. He flew the flak-filled missions, taking notes that formed the basis of his stories. And when he came home, he saw the struggle these vets experienced as they tried to readjust to civilian life. He wrote about that quiet and desperate battle back here in the States in his brilliant novel *Glory For Me*, which became the basis for the movie *The Best Years of Our Lives*. In it, Fred Derry, a bombardier with the 305th Bomb Group, serves as one of the three main characters. His words humanized the experience of a generation of aviators, and they will be quoted in the pages that follow.

As a kid, I would sneak into my father's den, which was filled with the beautiful and accurate models of the aircraft used in the strategic bombing campaign. He'd arrayed in one cabinet P-51s, P-38s, Focke-Wulfs, and Messerschmitts. I'd stare at them, fingers pressed to the glass, and let my imagination roam. Next to those cabinets, stored with military-like precision in stout bookshelves were hundreds of books and folios related to World War II aviation. Not allowed to touch them, they became my forbidden fruit. As soon as I was old enough to read, I would tiptoe inside Dad's den and pilfer a book or two, read it as quickly as I could and return it. Somehow, he always knew, and more than once I got busted. Nevertheless, from those stolen moments grew an abiding love of aviation history and the air war in Europe. Someday, I wanted to have the opportunity to write such volumes so that they may sit on Dad's shelf as well.

My childish and naïve view of the air war vanished in the 1990s when I interviewed hundreds of veterans of the Eighth and Fifteenth Air Forces. Through my time with them in their last few years, I saw their lingering pain; I heard their stories of friends trapped in jammed turrets that they were forced to leave behind as their bombers plunged broken and burning for the earth five miles below. In their words, in their tears for long-fallen comrades, and in their eyes I saw the true meaning of what took place during those seminal years seven decades ago. As a result, this book has been both a privilege and a passion to write—one of those projects that defines my own accomplishments in life. I hope every page honors their experience by staying honest to what they endured and why.

That is my gift to those men who took the time to trust me with me those jagged memories and open their wounded hearts to a young historian who knew nothing of the true nature of combat. Those moments, shared in their homes, shaped who I became and gave me purpose to my own life. This is their story, the view from their cockpits and turrets, told with all the raw honesty I gleaned from their words.

> And the fighters rolled into the tracer like rabbits,
> The blood froze over my splints like a scab—
> Did I snore, all still and grey in the turret,
> Till the palms rose out of the sea with my death?
> And the world ends here, in the sand of a grave,
> All my wars over? How easy it was to die!
> —*Randall Jarrell, Gunner*

The 549th Bomb Squadron returns from a mission to find coffee and donuts waiting for them, care of the Red Cross. Such gestures helped sustain the morale of those doing the flying and fighting. Through 1944, the Eighth Air Force's commander, Jimmy Doolittle, tried his best to give his airmen passes into the local English towns and cities so they could relax and unwind. Such consideration for his men landed Doolittle in hot water with his superiors, who were determined to ruthlessly prosecute the air war no matter how worn out the crews became.

Home safe. Come dawn, they'd have to fly again.

The craterscape of the Western Front left an indelible impression on the young officers who survived it. Never again, they vowed, would they send so many men to their deaths so pointlessly. Two schools of thought emerged from this ordeal. Some believed airpower alone could end the next war quickly. Others believed tanks and armored vehicles could restore mobility to the battlefield and deliver the war-winning blows with speed and movement.

I

A PANACEA FOR GENERATIONAL DESTRUCTION

⋆ ⋆ ⋆ ⋆ ⋆

There my adventurous ardor experienced a sobering shock. A fair-haired Scottish private was lying at the side of the trench in a pool of his own blood. His face was grey and serene, and his eyes stared emptily at the sky. A few yards further on the body of a German officer lay crumpled up and still . . . machine guns tapped, spiteful and spasmodic. High up in the fresh blue sky an aeroplane droned and glinted. I thought what a queer state of things it all was. . . .
—*Memoirs of an Infantry Officer*, Siegfried Sassoon

THE GREAT WAR CAME UPON EUROPE in the summer of 1914, sparked by an assassin's bullet and fueled by diplomatic miscalculations. Spurred by patriotic fever and images of glory and heroism in battle, legions of young men kissed their loved ones good-bye, stepped aboard troop trains across the Continent, and found themselves thrown into a new form of warfare nobody—from general to private—had ever envisioned.

They marched into battle in Napoleonic ranks. Instead of muskets, they faced Maxim machine guns and modern artillery. Garish uniforms, fit for striking impressions during the Bastille Day parades colored the French rank and file. The Zouaves wore blue and bright red pantaloons. Against the summer's earth, they made exceptional targets for German gunners, and they died in heaps.

During the Great War, airpower served an important supporting function on the Western Front. Reconnaissance, observation, and spotting for artillery units were the aircraft's most important duties. Here, an American 1st Aero Squadron Salmson recon aircraft soars above the front on a mission in 1918.

The concept of strategic bombing emerged from the traumatic experience of World War I's trench fighting. The machine gun, combined with long-range artillery, produced such appalling casualties that offensive operations could be conducted only at the expense of thousands of young lives for every mile of ground taken. When the Armistice was signed in 1918, the surviving professional officers took stock of what they'd just been through and sought ways to ensure such positional warfare would never happen again.

Charles DeGaulle (left) was one of the armor advocates in the French Army.

In the first three weeks of fighting on the Western Front, five hundred thousand men became casualties. Before the year was out, the French Army alone had suffered almost a million losses.

The war devolved into positional fighting where a few hundred yards of ground would be bought with the blood of thousands of young men. Through 1915, the loss rates only grew worse. Then came Verdun in February 1916, and the French Army all but succumbed to the flames of that crucible. Before the year was out, Verdun had claimed almost a million more men.

In June, the reconstituted British Army launched its offensive along the Somme River. After a week long artillery bombardment, the British infantry was expected to simply walk over whatever German resistance was left. Instead, as the men clambered out of their trenches and marched in orderly ranks through no man's land, they faced a hurricane of shrapnel and machine gun fire. By dusk, nineteen thousand British soldiers lay dead, some still lying in their parade ground ranks on the shell-savaged battlefield. Another forty thousand wounded overburdened the already inadequate medical evacuation pipeline, and their

continued on page 12

After the first British experiments with tanks on the battlefield, the French developed their own armored vehicles. Such first steps would give rise to the whole concept of combined arms—the integration of armor, infantry, and artillery into one powerful team on the battlefield. Colonel William Mitchell was the first—and, in the inter-war era, the only— airpower advocate who took the principle of combined arms operations and applied it to aviation. His tactical manual, written in the 1920s, was years ahead of its time as a result.

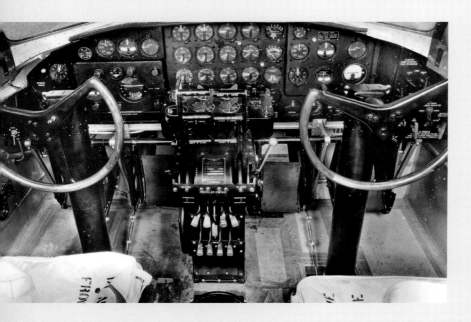

The Model 299's cockpit layout was not only one of the most complicated and technically challenging of the 1930s, but it was also well thought out and designed with the pilots in mind.

IN 1934, THE AIR CORPS issued a challenge to America's aircraft companies: build a revolutionary new bomber capable of flying for ten hours at 250 miles per hour while carrying thousands of pounds of ordnance. Three corporations, Boeing, Martin, and Douglas, rose to that challenge. The Air Corps scheduled a fly-off between whatever three planes the companies developed, and the winner would receive a contract for the construction of two hundred planes. Such a contract would ensure the survival of any one of these companies in the lean Depression-era years, and their best designers and engineers threw themselves into the task.

Douglas and Martin settled on twin-engine designs known as the DB-1 and the Model 146, respectively. Boeing, which had recently built the XB-15 and had experience with larger craft, decided to construct a prototype powered by four 750-horsepower motors, despite the fact that this would increase the individual cost of each aircraft significantly. Boeing's management believed that the extra engines gave their plane the performance edge they would need to secure the Air Corps contract.

In July 1935, Boeing's Model 299 took flight for the first time, armed with five .30-caliber machine guns. The test flight exceeded all hopes, and a month later it flew to Wright Field, Ohio, in under ten hours to take part in the performance competition against the DB-1 and Model 146.

In Ohio, the 299 crushed the opposition. It was faster, possessed

Above: The radioman's compartment in the Model 299. As the 299 evolved into the B-17, the aircraft eventually contained miles of electrical wiring and its generators could produce enough power to light a midsized town.

Left: A close-up of the Model 299's original nose turret. This was discarded in subsequent models. Initially replaced by hand-held .30-caliber and .50-caliber guns, the ultimate B-17, the G model, incorporated a chin turret with twin .50-caliber machine guns.

The arrival of the first YB-17 at Langley made the other aircraft on the field look positively primitive in comparison.

a longer range, and carried 4,800 pounds of bombs, while its defensive firepower was unmatched. At last, the Air Corps would have a true instrument of strategic bombing in its arsenal.

Yet, the contract ultimately went to Douglas. The DB-1 became the B-18 Bolo, and the Air Corps ordered 133 of them. Sixty-five Boeings were ordered as well, but then even that small amount got canceled when the Model 299 crashed in October during an evaluation flight. The crew had neglected to unlock the control surfaces before take-off, and the 299 nosed up, stalled, and augered in.

It looked like the end for the Boeing project. Nevertheless, enough Air Corps officers saw the potential that they steered some money toward Boeing the following year to build thirteen test aircraft, now designated as the YB-17. They cost almost a hundred thousand dollars apiece—a tremendous sum to the Air Corps at a time when military appropriations had been cut to the bone—but the YB-17s reached the 2nd Bomb Group in the spring of 1937. They came to the eager Air Corps crews complete with a number of improvements over the original

Model 299, including more powerful Wright-Cyclone engines and even heavier defensive armament.

The Air Corps loved the new bomber and saw it as the ultimate workhorse for the strategic bombing doctrine that dominated the service. Through 1938 and 1939, more were ordered in penny-packet amounts. Finally, as the war in Europe reached its first crisis in the summer of 1940 when France surrendered, Washington shook loose enough money to order just over five hundred B-17s. That first major contract set the stage for the aerial armada that would blacken the skies over Germany in a few short years. Yet, by the time the Japanese attacked Pearl Harbor, fewer than two hundred Flying Forts had reached operational status in the Air Corps.

By 1945, 12,731 B-17s had been produced by Boeing and Vega, a subsidiary of Lockheed. During the course of the war, Flying Forts dropped 640,000 tons of bombs on enemy targets, more than any other American aircraft. From its humble origins and near extinction in 1935, the B-17 rose to be the ultimate expression of strategic bombing during World War II.

continued from page 8

misery as they lay untended for hours or even days seems unimaginable now in a time when removing a casualty from the field takes a mere matter of minutes.

The pointless killing over ruined ground continued. The French Army nearly collapsed in mutiny. Units refused to charge headlong into German machine guns. Some bleated like sheep in their trenches when their officers ordered them to attack. Russia collapsed in revolution later in the year, and the Allied cause looked almost hopeless.

The Americans arrived in the nick of time. The French and British armies, scarred by four years of trench warfare, had not the heart to carry the day any longer. The Americans, unknowing and naïve, stormed into battle with the same élan seen in 1914. In a matter of weeks, 250,000 U.S. soldiers and marines fell during the summer and fall of 1918. In the end, the Americans gave the Allies the spirit and numbers to at last defeat the German army on the Western Front.

Above: Most postwar officers, especially from the older Victorian generation, did not see much potential in airpower. They saw fragile, fabric-covered aircraft like these German Fokker Dr. I fighters and focused on their limited range, armament, and combat payload. These early aircraft did not have the capability to win wars, but the reality of the day blinded many to the potential that lay in the future.

When the war finally ended in the famous railroad car at Compiègne, Europe's era of global dominance ended with it. Thirty million lives had been destroyed—eight million dead—in what became the bloodiest conflict in human history. The French mobilized 8.4 million men during the war; 5.7 million became casualties. Ninety percent of France's eighteen- to twenty-four-year-olds died or were maimed defending the trenches of the Western Front.

A generation had been all but wiped out. Aside from the United States, the warring nations lay in economic and social ruin. Entire villages in Britain, France, and Germany had been picked clean of its healthy sons. Now in the aftermath, only the elderly, infirm, or adolescent remained to move forward.

In the wake of the war, those junior officers who survived recognized the complete failure of the upper echelons of their chains of command, most of whom seemed unable to adapt to the convergence of new technology and dated tactics that took place on the Western Front. Some young turks, such as J. F. C. Fuller, D. H. Liddell-Hart, George Patton, and Charles DeGaulle, advocated the use of armor to restore mobility to the battlefield. They clashed with the old-school infantry and artillery officers who seemed incapable of understanding how squandering the youth of their nation in pointless frontal assaults had crippled their societies.

Left: Then there were men of extraordinary vision who embraced the airpower cause with almost zealot-like devotion. The most influential was Italy's rebellious Guilio Douhet. He believed airpower, if used to destroy an enemy nation's civilian morale through terror bombing, could bring a quick end to future wars.

The 1920s saw the first steps toward creating a bomber force capable of realizing Douhet's bloody vision. Here, American MB-2 bombers pass over New York. From these dope-and-fabric-covered fragile craft would spring the deadly effective weapons of the following decade.

Other military rebels rose to prominence in the early 1920s. These renegades believed technology had made armies all but obsolete, and that the next war would be won not by rifle and bayonet, but by aircraft.

Enter the airpower zealots. One of the first of these was the Italian Giulio Douhet. In 1911, during the Italo-Turkish War, he glimpsed the potential of the aircraft as an offensive weapon of war. He commanded an air battalion in North Africa and during his stint in the desert penned one of the very first air battle manuals ever written.

During the Great War, Douhet relentlessly advocated for a massive bomber force that could devastate Italy's enemies. He bombarded his superiors and senior governmental officials for such an expansion program. Simultaneously, he castigated the Italian army for its ineptitude and unpreparedness.

All this agitation managed only to get him court-martialed and thrown in prison for a year. In 1917, after Italy suffered staggering losses during the Battle of Caporetto, the Italian military released him from his cell and made him central director of aviation at the General Air Commisariat. He continued to be an agitator and drove his superiors nuts with his persistent demands and complete lack of a political filter. He said what he felt, didn't care who took offense, and flamed out yet again. This time, he resigned from the Italian Army and turned his attention to writing.

In 1921, he published what would become the single most influential book on military airpower for the next thirty years. Seen through the lens of twenty-first-century warfare and the pains Western militaries take to minimize civilian losses, Douhet's book is nothing short of an apocalyptic vision of societal destruction through aerial bombardment.

Billy Mitchell in the cockpit of a Thomas-Morse Scout. Mitchell was not an exclusive advocate of strategic bombing. He was an advocate of airpower in general and its balanced employment on the battlefield. Abrasive, visionary, devoted to the cause of an independent air service with visceral devotion, he was the army's ultimate rebel during the 1920s. It cost him his career, but his teaching and influence defined the United States Army Air Corps for generations to come.

Mitchell made national headlines when he unleashed an assault on the navy's sacred cow: the battleship. In a series of tests, he proved conclusively that aircraft could sink any armored vessel, both with direct hits as well as near misses that shattered hulls with their hammer-like concussion waves. What seems obvious now was not to hide-bound, tradition-impaired elderly flag officers who dominated the upper echelons of the navy during the 1920s. They spent much of the decade trying to marginalize the tests.

The Navy invested millions of dollars into its lighter-than-air program during the 1920s and 1930s. For the most part, it was wasted effort. Rigid airships like the USS *Shenandoah*, *Akron*, and *Macon* had no place on the modern battlefield. The infrastructure to support these massive aerial giants survived their demise to be used in a variety of roles in the decades to come. Here, the massive rigid airship hangar at Moffett Field, California, became home to squadrons of anti-submarine blimps used by the navy to patrol the west coast. The hangar was so huge it developed its own weather systems. It is still in existence today.

Douhet believed that the next war would see armies stalemated in murderous trench fighting once again. As men flung themselves into raining artillery shells and sweeping machine gun fire, Douhet envisioned the ultimate victory would be the nation that devoted its resources toward the construction of an offensive air force. With the deadlock claiming thousands below, fleets of bombers would soar over the front to first secure command of the air. With the enemy's air units destroyed through bombing of their airfields and production infrastructure, the victor could turn its attention to carpet-bombing cities, communication centers, and vital targets. Kill women, children, the factory workers who built the planes, tanks, and rifles used on the front lines, and the war would be won. Douhet's cold calculations even called for drenching already stricken cities with poison gas to kill its first responders and security forces as they sought to save trapped citizens and restore order.

It was the ultimate vision of total warfare. No longer would the rifle-armed soldier be in the crosshairs. For Douhet, the answer to World War I's gruesome toll was to traumatize a society so completely that its terrorized citizens would rise up in revolution, sweep away their government, and sue for peace. The airplane and the aerial bomb would be the delivery system for slaying national morale and resolve to continue the fighting.

Through the 1920s, Douhet's book gained traction slowly throughout Europe. In France, while some air-minded officers became followers of Douhet, the French military establishment gradually let the L'Armee de L'Air waste away to a skeleton of its former 1918 glory and instead devoted its budget to building the Maginot Line. To the French Army, concrete seemed to be the answer to positional warfare. In Britain, however, the independent Royal Air Force had been searching for a unique role. Douhet's concepts gave the RAF a raison d'etre and dovetailed with thinking already developing in that service. Hugh "Boom" Trenchard, the commander of the RAF, saw strategic bombing as the saving grace for his

When the navy's airship USS *Shenandoah* went down in 1925, Mitchell used the event to publically excoriate his superiors in Washington, D.C. Such an assault could not go unpunished, and Mitchell was court-martialed. The trial ended his military career.

George Kenney, who would latter gain fame as the commander of General Douglas MacArthur's Far Eastern Air Forces, had spent much of his career in the 1920s focused on tactical aviation. He innovated and developed a number of tactics and weapons to support such operations. Ironically, he was the officer who translated Douhet's seminal work on strategic bombing, *Command of the Air* into English and brought it to an American audience.

beloved independent branch of the British military and used that concept as a way to maintain what slender appropriations were available to national defense through the 1920s.

In the United States, Gen. William "Billy" Mitchell dominated the nascent air service. Mitchell was one of those officers who generated enormous passion around him. His dynamic leadership and vision attracted many acolytes, including men like Henry "Hap" Arnold and Carl Spaatz. At the same time, Mitchell possessed a knack for alienating his superiors and the politically influential with his blunt talk and willingness to speak his mind. In that respect, he and Douhet were kindred spirits, and Mitchell never backed away from a fight if it furthered the cause of military airpower in the United States.

In 1921, Mitchell took on the U.S. Navy establishment and slaughtered that service's sacred cow: the battleship. In a series of tests, he proved that aircraft could sink what had been up to that point the foremost expression of military power projection. Mitchell went on to write a treatise on airpower doctrine that he called *Notes on the Multi-Motored Bombardment Group Day and Night*. In most respects, it was more sophisticated and down-to-earth than Douhet's grand vision of the future. Douhet didn't sweat the details; Mitchell, who had commanded a force of almost a thousand planes at the end of World War I, kept his ideas rooted in operational realities. As a result, his doctrine believed that firm cooperation between bomber and fighter groups would be the only way to defeat an enemy's air force. As a former infantryman, he became the first of the airpower visionaries to integrate combined operations between the two types of combat aircraft.

Unfortunately, before he could mold the U.S. Air Service in his image, his mouth earned him an E-ticket ride into retirement. In September 1925, the U.S. Navy's airship,

continued on page 20

The early 1930s saw the United States Army Air Corps receive some of its first modern and homegrown aircraft designs. The American aeronautical industry had made tremendous gains after its rocky performance during World War I. Here, a squadron of Martin B-10 bombers sit on a parking ramp at March Field in 1934. Fast and well-armed, the B-10 represented a huge technological leap for the United States and helped pave the way for the superb aircraft that would help win the war.

THE NORDEN BOMBSIGHT

DEVELOPED BY THE CARL NORDEN, a Dutch engineer and entrepreneur who cut his teeth in the aviation business at the Sperry Corporation, the Norden bombsight gained tremendous fame before and during World War II as one of the most accurate devices of its kind. Press reports claimed it could place a bomb in a pickle barrel from 20,000 feet. The Air Corps valued its accuracy so much that it became one of the most sensitive items in its inventory, a closely guarded secret device that bombardiers were sworn to destroy should their planes go down in enemy territory. Ironically, a German spy who worked at Sperry stole the design data for the Norden bombsight and passed it back to the Third Reich as early as 1938.

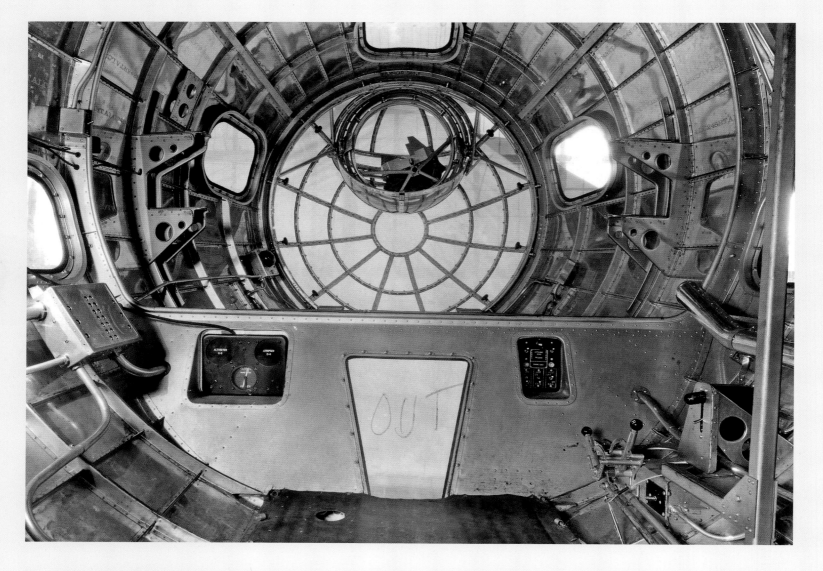

The nose of the Model 299. For this strategic bomber to reach its full potential, the aircraft had to be married with an ordnance delivery system that could effectively put bombs on target. This was easier said than done and required a technological revolution in bombsight design to achieve.

The Norden bombsight was that technological revolution. Essentially, it functioned as a primitive analog computer. The USAAC was so paranoid that it might fall into foreign hands that bombardiers had to swear they would destroy it if they were about to be shot down. Ironically, the Germans stole the design in the 1930s, so the whole secrecy operation had been compromised long before the Norden went into battle for the first time.

The secret behind the Norden bombsight's accuracy was its ability to compute wind drift and ground speed. Working in conjunction with an autopilot system, the bombardier actually controlled his aircraft's movements during the final approach to target through inputs to the autopilot via the Norden sight.

The Air Corps believed that this gave its bombardment groups the final tool necessary to carry out long-range pinpoint bombing. With such an accurate sight, no factory would be safe from the bombs carried aloft by the new B-17 Flying Fortresses. Civilian casualties could be minimized, and the accuracy would allow the Air Corps a measure of economy of force Douhet's carpet bombing theories never would have allowed.

In practice, the Norden sight did prove more accurate than most of its contemporaries, but a variety of factors still made hitting a target from 20,000 feet extraordinarily difficult. A B-17 on its bomb run traveled at least 350 feet per second. In combat, the Eighth and Fifteenth Air Force groups learned early on that it was tactically impossible for every plane in the formation to aim and bomb independently. That had been tried during the North African campaign, but it broke up formations and made the bombers vulnerable to Luftwaffe fighters. As a result, each group dropped its bombs when the lead bombardier released.

A B-17 bombardier sits in his office. The USAAF's belief in the accuracy of the Norden bombsight made the entire concept of daylight pinpoint bombing possible. While in the field under combat conditions, the Norden sight did not perform nearly as well as advertised, it was still one of the most accurate devices of its day.

In the few seconds it would take for the other bombardiers to toggle their loads, the B-17s would have traveled hundreds, if not thousands of feet beyond the initial drop point, causing a wide pattern on the ground.

Other factors limited accuracy as well. The bombs themselves were aerodynamically unpredictable. The weight of the paint on the bomb affected its fall. When different paints were used, the trajectories were affected as well. In the end, pinpoint bombing would have to wait until the advent of laser-guided weaponry in the 1970s. The best the Norden bombsight could do during World War II was get half the bombs dropped within a quarter mile of the target area.

The Douglas B-18 Bolo served as the first conceived and purpose-built strategic bomber for the USAAC. It possessed many drawbacks, including a light payload and short radius of action.

USS *Shenandoah*, went down in a Midwest storm, killing fourteen members of its crew. Mitchell used the disaster to excoriate the defense establishment's leadership, calling his superiors "criminally negligent."

Mitchell's bomb-throwing in the press landed him in front of court-martial board, which ultimately found him guilty of "conduct prejudicial to good order and discipline" despite the fact that many of his acolytes, Arnold and Spaatz included, testified on his behalf. Sentenced to five years suspension from active duty, Mitchell instead resigned his commission, his career over. During the final years of his life, he grew increasingly shrill with his attacks on the army and his agitation for an independent air force along the British lines.

Mitchell may have flamed out just like Douhet, but his ideas had taken root. His devotees proved much more patient and politically adept. In the years that followed, they worked within the system to see much of Mitchell's vision actually get implemented.

In 1933, George Kenney, who had been one of the few American advocates of low-level tactical bombing, translated Douhet's *Command of the Air* into English. The book spread

A YB-17 Flying Fortress over the Cascade Mountains. Though the B-17 program initially lost out to the cheaper B-18, the USAAC saw so much potential in the design that funds were made available to continue developing it.

through the Air Corps like a wildfire. At the Tactical School, which had been established in 1931 at Maxwell Field, Alabama, Douhet's theories soon formed the core of the syllabus taught to an entire generation of aviators. Lieutenant Colonel Don Wilson, the curriculum director at Maxwell, added his own twist that became the signature of American strategic bombing doctrine in the years to come.

Wilson read Douhet and found his total disregard for civilian life to be appalling. Why was it necessary to replace the slaughter in the trenches with mass slaughter in the streets of an enemy's cities? Instead, Wilson advocated focusing bombing attacks on vital targets. Instead of raining bombs down on urban centers, the Tactical School taught the focused application of bombing against key industrial targets. Along the way, Mitchell's belief that combined fighter and bomber operations lost favor. The strategic bomber became the be-all and end-all to the U.S. Army Air Corps's mission for the next war.

A B-10 during a flight to Alaska in 1934.

From that was born the concept of pinpoint bombing, carried out by multi-engined, long-range aircraft that possessed enough defensive firepower to defeat any enemy interceptors launched at them. Through the 1930s, the Army Air Corps strived to develop the tools needed for such a mission. The two critical components—an aircraft with the capability to undertake the mission and a bomb sight that could deliver ordnance on target accurately—came together in the late 1930s with the arrival of the Boeing B-17 Flying Fortress and the Norden Bombsight. These two remarkable innovations placed the United States on the leading edge of long-range bombing technology just as the war in Europe broke out in 1939. Finally, the airpower advocates had the tools to see their vision realized.

In Poland, the Ju-87 Stuka dive-bomber earned a fearsome reputation within the Polish rank and file. Deadly accurate in its dive, the Stuka crews affixed sirens to their aircraft and they would shriek down out of the sky to deliver their bombs on Polish troop and vehicle convoys. Such attacks helped break the spirit of Poland's defenders.

2

THEORY INTO PRACTICE

I was the first correspondent to reach Guernica, and was immediately pressed into service by some Basque soldiers collecting charred bodies that the flames had passed over. Some of the soldiers were sobbing like children. There were flames and smoke and grit, and the smell of burning human flesh was nauseating. Houses were collapsing into the inferno.
—*Noel Monks,* London Daily Express, *1937*

THE BOMBERS THUNDERED OVERHEAD sometime after lunch on an April day in 1937. Curious Basque citizens turned their faces skyward to see orderly formations of twin-engine aircraft paraded overhead, shepherded along by an equal number of fighters. Curiosity turned to terror when the bombs began to fall. Panic stricken, the men, women, and children of Guernica fled the streets for the sanctuary of cellars and stout-walled buildings.

Messerschmitt Bf-109s and Fiat CR-32s swept down on the town to strafe those who attempted to fly the town and gain refuge in the countryside beyond. It was cold-blooded murder, and it lasted for almost four hours. When the German and Italian planes finally turned for home, Guernica burned virtually to the last building. In the ashes lay the corpses of 1,650 civilians.

One of the first fast twin-engine bombers produced by a resurgent Germany in the 1930s was the Junkers Ju-86. Such aircraft helped destroy Guernica during the Luftwaffe's terror bombing experiment in the Spanish Civil War.

Wolfram von Richthofen, seen here on the Eastern Front during World War II, conceived and executed the terror raid on Guernica and was quite pleased with the subsequent results.

Following the experiment at Guernica, the beautiful city of Barcelona became the next terror bombing test case. Hundreds more civilians died as Italian aircraft pummeled the city with bombs. These two attacks helped convinced the Luftwaffe's leadership that Douhet's theories had merit. They set the stage for Warsaw, Rotterdam, and the London Blitz.

Noel Monks, a daring war correspondent who would later spend time in France with the RAF during the Phony War and beyond, later wrote in his memoir, *Eyewitness*, "A sight that haunted me for weeks was the charred bodies of several women and children huddled together in what had been the cellar of a house."

The Germans and their Nationalist Spanish allies denied any involvement in the attack. It was not until 1999 that the German government formerly acknowledged the Luftwaffe's role and apologized for what took place there that day in 1937.

In the midst of the Spanish Civil War, the Luftwaffe's leadership had decided to test Guilio Douhet's nihilistic vision of terror bombing. The people of Guernica did not know it, but they had been selected as the guinea pigs for this doctrinal experiment. Families died, children burned alive as flames consumed their homes, and in a secret report, Condor Legion commander Wolfram von Richthofen declared the attack to be a tremendous success. The will of the survivors in Guernica had been broken.

Adolf Hitler offers a warm greeting to Reichsmarschal Hermann Goering, commander of the new Luftwaffe. The German air force's performance in Poland and the Battle of France sent Goering's political influence soaring. Only after the Battle of Britain did his standing erode in his Fuehrer's eyes.

German troops fight their way into a Polish village during the initial invasion in September 1939. The Poles fought valiantly, but they were overmatched against the more modern Nazi war machine. The Luftwaffe's tactical air support, combined with its terror bombing of Warsaw, played a key role in the Polish defeat.

German officers in a field headquarters coordinate and set the tempo of the battle flow in Poland. Coordination between the forward units and the Luftwaffe proved to be very difficult, but also of tremendous value in crushing opposition with minimal losses in return.

Polish troops fought fiercely and inflicted heavy losses at times on the German Wehrmacht. But when the Soviets invaded Eastern Poland, the soldiers lost all hope. Crushed on both flanks, the Poles surrendered Warsaw, and the war ended a few days later.

The Stuka's fixed gear, slow speed, and lack of armament became manifestly obvious as soon as its crews faced a determined and modern air force. Against the Poles, French, Belgians, Dutch, Danes, and Norwegians, however, the Ju-87 served up stark terror to its targets.

The Junkers Ju-88, the fastest twin-engine bomber then in service, saw extensive combat over Poland, France, and the Low Countries. Used both as a level bomber and a dive-bomber, the Ju-88 later found another niche as a night fighter. It became the mainstay of the Luftwaffe's nocturnal interceptor force along with the Messerschmitt Bf-110.

Two years later, Adolf Hitler's Wehrmacht invaded Poland, a move that triggered France and Britain to declare war on Germany. For the second time in twenty years, Europe descended into the nightmare of another general war.

Though the Luftwaffe had developed mainly into a close support force, Wolfram von Ricthofen's Douhetesque experiment at Guernica was taken to heart. From the outset of the fighting, the Luftwaffe conducted terror raids against the Polish capital. Civilians were strafed by passing fighters. Heinkel He-111s and Dornier Do-17s pummeled Warsaw daily with bombs. On September 10, 1939, they flew seventeen raids against the city and caused so much havoc the residents referred to that day as "Bloody Sunday" afterwards. The Germans ignored many choice military targets, such as Polish Army barracks and army facilities around the capital, choosing instead to stick with Douhet's playbook.

Defended by a hundred thousand desperate and courageous Polish soldiers, Warsaw held out for over a week in the face of overwhelming German forces. As the siege progressed, the Poles even managed to counterattack and push the Wehrmacht back in places. Hitler turned to the Luftwaffe to break the siege. Von Richthofen wanted to burn the capital to the ground, making it fit only as a "customs station" in the future. Terror would bring the Poles to their knees.

continued on page 35

Right: A close-up of a Messerschmitt Bf-109's nose. The 109 possessed an excellent rate of climb and a slight speed advantage over its most capable adversaries, including the French D.520 and British Spitfire. Its extremely short endurance made it an impractical escort fighter.

Ju-87 Stuka crews study maps in the final minutes before a mission against targets in Norway. Airpower played a vital role in Nazi Germany's successful campaign in Scandinavia.

The wrecked remains of Polish bombers, seen in the aftermath of the first campaign of World War II.

The German Army, though largely composed of infantry dependent on horse-drawn transport, did possess a thoroughly modern armored force. Used en masse at weak points along enemy defensive lines, the panzers achieved numerous critical breakthroughs during the campaigns of 1939 and 1940. Without the panzer menace, it is quite possible the terror bombing unleashed on Poland and Holland would not have had the effect that it did.

A painting of a German bomber pilot. Thanks to their combat tours in Spain during the Civil War, Luftwaffe air crews were among the most experienced and well-trained in the world in 1940.

German troops react to incoming artillery fire. In the 1939 and 1940 campaigns, the Wehrmacht defeated its opponents through superior organization and better integration of airpower into the land war. Without the Luftwaffe, these early victories would not have been possible.

A formation of Bristol Blenheim RAF bombers. The Blenheim was one of the most numerous twin-engine strike craft in the British arsenal at the start of the war. Early attacks on German naval bases in broad daylight resulted in heavy Blenheim losses and helped convince the RAF high command to switch to night bombing.

To conquer Holland, the Germans used daring tactical operations that gained strategic results. This included the airborne assault on Fort Eben-Emael, a key defensive complex that could have held up the main German invasion force for many days. Instead, fewer than a hundred German paratroopers—including the ones seen here—landed atop the fort and captured it in a surprise coup de main. Such an operation would never have been possible had not the Luftwaffe owned the skies over Holland from the outset of the 1940 campaign.

THE FRENCH AIR FORCE IN WORLD WAR II: TOO LITTLE, TOO LATE

France attempted to nationalize its aircraft industry in the mid-1930s. The results were absolutely disastrous and played a major role in the nation's humiliating defeat in 1940. After the industry was nationalized, production plummeted, work on new designs languished, and innovation, once a hallmark of French aviation, atrophied. In 1939, the situation was so desperate that the country that armed the United States' fledgling air service in 1917–1918 had to look across the Atlantic for help. The L'Armee de L'Air purchased hundreds of American-built aircraft, including Curtiss Hawk 75A fighters.

This stopgap effort proved to be too little, too late. When the Germans invaded in 1940, the French Air Force was still a shadow of its former world-leading self. It lacked a first-rate, modern fighter that could stand against the Bf-109. Most of its bomber force flew ancient or outdated aircraft. The Amiot 143, designed for both bombing and reconnaissance, was slow, ugly, and vulnerable. The medium bombers were easy meat for hunting Bf-109s and Bf-110s.

The most modern bomber available to the French in 1940 was the LeO 451. Fast with clean lines and heavy defensive armament for its time, the LeO 451 could have been a major offensive addition to the Allied arsenal if it had been deployed in greater numbers. Instead, the French went to war with a largely antiquated fleet of bombers.

The Dewoitine D.520, a newly designed fighter, saw service in very small numbers during the Battle of France. Though a great leap forward over the Morane 406 and Bloch MB-152 fighters then in front line service, the D.520 actually ended up serving the Axis powers much longer than it did the Allies. The Germans used it as a trainer; the Vichy French ended up fielding several squadrons of them, and others found their way into the hands of some of the lesser Axis nations as point defense interceptors.

The French airpower disaster remains one of the most complete defeats in aviation history. Though its brave fighter pilots did take a steady toll on the Luftwaffe, the L'Armee de L'Air suffered a complete strategic defeat at the hands of a tactically focused air force.

American Curtiss Hawk 75A fighters purchased by the French Air Force in a last-minute effort to modernize their outdated and underpopulated arsenal.

The Lioré et Olivier LeO 451 was a relatively modern bomber design, but production delays minimized its impact on the war.

The Dewoitine D.520, although slower than the German Bf-109, was more maneuverable, if somewhat erratic to control. As with the LeO 451, production difficulties limited its numbers.

With design roots stretching back to the late 1920s, the ungainly Amiot 143 was far outclassed by the German aircraft it had to go up against.

By concentrating its panzer divisions in the lightly guarded Ardennes sector of the Western Front, the Germans were able to rupture the Allied lines and cut much of the Anglo-French Army off in Belgium. This forced the Allies to withdraw over three hundred thousand men from the continent at Dunkirk. That disaster presaged the complete collapse of France and its surrender after forty days of fighting.

A true multinational effort. American-built, French-flown Hawk 75 fighters escort a formation of RAF Fairey Battle light attack bombers. The Fairey Battle squadrons in France were virtually wiped out in the fighting following the German invasion of the West in May 1940.

On September 25, 1939, the Luftwaffe launched over a thousand bomber sorties against Warsaw. Five hundred tons of explosives and incendiaries leveled entire blocks. Hospitals, schools, waterworks, and once-quiet neighborhood streets grew choked with rubble and dying civilians. The situation became intolerable. The next day, the Poles explored surrender options rather than let the slaughter of its people in Warsaw continue.

The following spring, when the Germans invaded Norway, the Low Countries, and France, the Luftwaffe employed terror bombing once again, this time to break the will of the Dutch to carry on fighting by flattening the last major industrial city not under German control. The Dutch troops defending the city were given an ultimatum to surrender or face aerial destruction. Just as the ground force commander accepted the ultimatum, the German bombers arrived. Some received a hastily sent abort order, but most did not, and downtown Rotterdam crumbled to burnt ruins under a rain of bombs.

continued on page 41

German citizens look over the wreckage of two Allied bombers shot down during the 1940 campaign. In the background are the skeletal remains of a Vickers Wellington, the mainstay of Bomber Command's long-range squadrons in 1940. In the foreground are the twisted pieces of a French Amiot 143, one of the ugliest and most vulnerable bombers deployed in any number during World War II. These same curious citizens would experience the full horrors of terror bombing in the years to come.

German troops at Narvik hunker down in the snow during a British air attack. The Norway campaign was anything but an easy one for the Third Reich. Stretched to the limit of its logistical capacity to pull the invasion off, the ground forces ultimately depended on the Luftwaffe's control of the air for close support and resupply missions, especially after the German Navy was so badly mauled in the initial invasion.

The first major strategic airlift of the war came in support of the Norway operation. The Luftwaffe, using Junkers 52 transports like the ones seen here, seized airfields with loads of troops, then brought in supplies to keep the men well provisioned with food and ammunition. It was an example of the strategic flexibility airpower offered whoever controlled the skies.

A Ju-52 tows a glider, much like the ones used to seize Fort Eben-Emael in Belgium during the assault on the Low Countries.

Hauptmann Hozzel, a well-decorated Stuka leader, poses for the camera in Norway. With the strategic seizure of airfields, the Luftwaffe was able to forward deploy close support units that helped defeat the Allied forces in the Narvik area.

The German panzer divisions poured out of the Ardennes and captured the strategically vital town of Sedan on their way to the Channel Coast. It was a significant moment, as the French had been defeated here in 1871 during the Franco-Prussian War, and the memory of that disaster lingered in the French consciousness. Seeing Sedan fall again came as a blow to national morale.

The aftermath of the fighting around Dunkirk. A British anti-tank unit has been wiped out by roving panzers.

The Potez 63.11 multi-role aircraft came in reconnaissance, light attack, night fighter, and heavy fighter variants. Hampered by ineffectual engines that lacked power, the Potez series was another failed French design. Most were destroyed in 1940, but enough survived to equip several Vichy squadrons in North Africa, where they were encountered by the United States during the Torch campaign in 1942.

The Germans march under the Arc de Triomphe in June 1940. With Paris in the Third Reich's hands, the French cause unraveled, and its government sued for peace. It was the lowest point in France's long and storied military history.

German pilots confer over a map prior to another mission in the West. After the fall of France, Britain fell squarely in the Luftwaffe's crosshairs, setting the stage for the first pure air campaign in history.

Dutch Fokker DXXI fixed-geared fighters in formation. Light and agile, these well-built fighters lacked the speed of the Bf-109 and could not hold its own against the Luftwaffe's more modern designed. However, some of them did see service with the Finnish Air Force in the 1939–1940 Winter War and took a heavy toll of Soviet Red Air Force aircraft. Over Holland the following spring, however, the Fokker squadrons could not hope to retain command of the air against the Luftwaffe's superior numbers and more advanced fighters.

A few days later, the Germans threatened to the bomb Utrecht if the Dutch government did not surrender. Without an air force left to defend its skies from such an onslaught, the Netherlands accepted defeat and fell beneath the Nazi jackboot.

Terror bombing succeeded once again.

Against France, the Luftwaffe unleashed a concerted attack against the L'Armee de L'Air's infrastructure. Waves of Dorniers, Heinkels, and Junkers bombers unleashed their full fury upon the French airfields and air depots. The French, whose aviation production system had all but collapsed at the end of the 1930s when the Socialists nationalized the aircraft companies, fought valiantly with obsolete equipment that the Germans simply shot out of the sky. The French managed to take a heavy toll of the attacking Luftwaffe planes, but simply did not have the numbers or the quality to stand and fight for long. Within days, the Germans had secured Douhet's Holy Grail: command of the air. The British Army evacuated the Continent at Dunkirk, and the French did not stand a chance. After forty days of fighting, they surrendered to Hitler in the same railroad car that ended World War I.

Britain now stood alone.

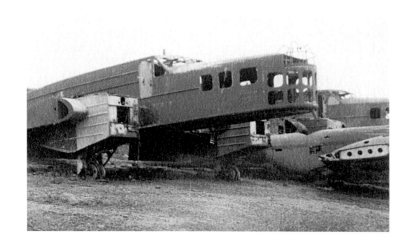

The French airpower disaster remains one of the most complete defeats in aviation history. Though its brave fighter pilots did take a steady toll on the Luftwaffe, the L'Armee de L'Air suffered a complete strategic defeat at the hands of a tactically focused air force.

A Hurricane IIC with 20mm cannon. The Hurricane's robust strength and relative ease of construction made it indispensable during the Battle of Britain.

3

THE SUMMER OF THE FEW

★ ★ ★ ★ ★

Once coming back from the gates with some fresh water to drink and to steep the handkerchiefs which we had tied across our faces against the colossal heat, I saw our hoses disappearing into the smoke and flame where we were working. I suddenly felt cut off and alone. I thought, "How bloody hopeless—all London's alight."
---—Firefighter Louis Abbot Wilson

Up on the top floor of the gynecological ward, we had fifteen women we couldn't move. They stayed in their beds through it all without complaint, although a bomb smashed the staff quarters next door, covering them with glass from their windows and plaster from the ceiling. In another wing, we had to leave another dozen fracture cases. All night long, they lay on their backs, unable to move, hung up on their frames and watched the Jerry planes cruising about the fire lit sky through a huge hole that had been blown out of the wall. The effect was stupefying.
—Dr. Harry Winter, Coventry

Dornier Do-17 "Flying Pencils" equipped much of the Luftwaffe's bomber force in the summer of 1940. During the Spanish Civil War, the Dornier was faster than most of the Republican interceptors trying to shoot it down. That experience seemed to vindicate the Dornier's design philosophy, which sacrificed armament and armor for speed. Over England, the Do-17 crews faced first-line fighters like the Hurricane and Spitfire for the first time. Unable to run away from interception, their lack of heavy defensive weaponry became a significant weakness that led to a lot of casualties.

JULY 10, 1940. The Luftwaffe bombers formed up over Pas de Calais, twenty-six strong from the crack Kampfgeschwader KG-2. The crews manning KG-2's Dornier Do-17Z "Flying Pencils" first cut their teeth in combat over Poland the previous fall. Some had even flown missions with the Condor Legion. Seasoned, capable veterans, they arrayed themselves into tight Vs and sped across the Channel, bound for a convoy an earlier reconnaissance mission discovered churning through the

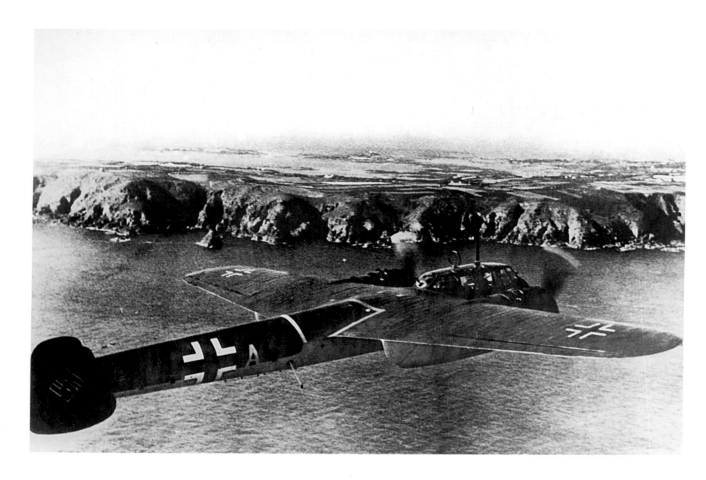

The Luftwaffe deployed three twin-engined tactical bombers during the Battle of Britain, including the Do-17, the Heinkel He-111, and the Junkers Ju-88. The Dornier Do-17 was the workhorse, but its design weaknesses led it to be phased out of front-line service over the next two years. Different variants did function as night interceptors, including the Do-217, but the Battle of Britain was the Dornier's operational peak in its originally intended role.

waters of the Thames Estuary. En route, they linked up with no fewer than five squadrons of escorting Bf-110 and Bf-109 fighters. They would be the shield, guarding the Dorniers from any RAF interceptors that rose to challenge them.

British radar stations detected the inbound raid. Already, six Hurricane fighters patrolled over the convoy, but clearly they would not be enough to handle the size of the attacking force. The radar sites reported this development up the chain of command. Eleven Group scrambled seven Hurricanes from B Flight, 56 Squadron. This was the legendary element led by ace Jimmy McCudden, who fought an epic battle with forty-eight-kill Werner Voss in 1917. Now, a new generation of British pilots would swarm into battle with the legacy of their squadron's elite heritage riding their shoulders.

At nearby Manston, a flight of Spitfires from 74 "Tiger" Squadron stood on the runway, cocked and locked, waiting for the order to scramble. In minutes, they too took to the skies and sped for the Thames Estuary.

In 1940, Fighter Command included a number of international squadrons. Pilots whose nations had been overrun by the Germans made their way to England to continue the fight. In combat, they displayed tenacious resolve as they sought vengeance against those who conquered their homelands. Here, Belgian pilots in the RAF cluster around a Hurricane's cockpit.

The Messerschmitt Bf-110 Zestroyer joined the Luftwaffe as its first heavy fighter. Designed to be a fast, powerfully armed stablemate of the Bf-109, the 110 lacked the maneuverability to effectively defeat front-line fighters like the Spitfire or Hurricane. During the 1939–1940 campaign, the lack of quality opposition masked its weaknesses in air combat. Over England, Fighter Command feasted on the 110 geschwaders and inflicted sharp losses on them. Nevertheless, the Bf-110 was the only Luftwaffe fighter capable of long-range escort missions, and it remained in the forefront of the fight throughout the Battle of Britain.

The Hawker Hurricane formed the backbone of RAF Fighter Command. The first British fighter capable of reaching speeds over 300 miles per hour, the Hurricane entered service in the late 1930s as the RAF's first monoplane fighter. Armed with eight .303-caliber machine guns, four in each wing, the British originally believed it was quite heavily armed. Combat against German bombers convinced Fighter Command that the .303s lacked the punch needed to bring such aircraft down. Later versions of the Hurricane came equipped with four 20mm cannons as a result.

Concentrated firepower was the Bf-110's greatest asset. Four 7.9mm machine guns and two 20mm cannons filled the aircraft's nose, making it one of the most heavily armed fighters in action in 1940. Despite this advantage, its lack of maneuverability often made the 110 a liability in the skies over England. Eventually, it would find its niche as a night fighter and would equip most of the nachtjaeger geschwarders tasked with defending the Reich from RAF bombers.

At Croydon, only a few miles from Dover, all available Hurricanes from 111 Squadron launched within minutes of receiving news of the incoming strike. Their nine fighters took station in a long, shallow V. They would employ a particularly terrifying tactic on this day to bring down the Luftwaffe's bombers.

Over the convoy, 111 Squadron spotted the onrushing Flying Pencils. The Hurricane pilots rolled into the attack: nine against twenty-six in a furious head-on pass with a closure rate of over five hundred miles an hour. The Croydon boys were only one of two outfits to practice this sort of daring maneuver in 11 Group. It required steel nerves and cat-quick reflexes to pull off successfully.

A Luftwaffe bomber crew jokes around
during a final pre-flight moment during the
Battle of Britain.

At the outset of the Battle of Britain, much of
the air combat took place over the English
Channel. The Luftwaffe fighter and bomber
crews were amply supplied with survival
gear, and air-sea rescue float planes and
flying boats were deployed to the French and
Belgian coasts to pick up crews who
force-landed in the Channel. Ironically,
the Germans were better prepared than the
British on that front, and it would take
several weeks and supreme effort for the
British to organize an effective way to
recover pilots who ended up in the water.

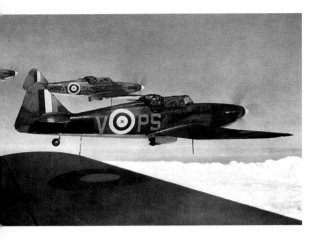

The Defiant represented serious error in tactical design judgment within the RAF during the mid-1930s. Conceived as a two-seat fighter that allowed the pilot to focus on flying and the gunner to focus on shooting, the Defiant carried only four .303 Browning machine guns in the turret. Without any forward-firing armament, and the weight of the turret inhibiting speed and maneuverability, the Defiant squadrons quickly discovered they stood virtually no chance against the Bf-109.

The Defiant later saw service as one of the first RAF night fighters, using their turret guns to fire upward into Luftwaffe bombers from below. Lacking a radar system, it was at best a stopgap, and the aircraft was later relegated to target towing duties after other, more effective night fighters like the Bristol Beaufighter arrived in strength.

The two formations merged, the Hurricanes' seventy-two .303-caliber machine guns spewing tracers into KG-2's Dorniers. The steady veteran pilots behind the controls of the German bombers reeled at the attack. Their orderly Vs disintegrated as they dodged and weaved the incoming fire. The British timed their attack perfectly; the Germans had been on the final stages of the bomb run. As they scattered to avoid the Hurricanes, their payloads fell all over the estuary. Of the 150 bombs dropped, only one scored a hit on the convoy. The daring head-on pass of 111 Squadron had just saved scores of sailors' lives.

In seconds, their Hurricanes flashed past, going flat-out below or above the bomber formation. One RAF pilot, Flight Officer T. P. K. Higgs, misjudged his run—an easy thing to do with such a pass. His Hurricane careened into the lead Do-17. Both planes exploded, their remains streaming for the estuary below. Miraculously, the Luftwaffe's staffel leader, Hauptmann Walter Krieger and one other crewman survived the fall into the water. They were fished out by the British and taken prisoner. Higgs died in the collision.

The remaining eight Hurricanes swung around to make another pass. At the same time, the German fighter escort sped to the rescue, caught one of the 111 Squadron pilots, Flight Officer Henry Ferris, as he shot down a Bf-109. Three more Messerschmitts latched onto his tail, their machine guns chewing through his aileron control. He dove for home and raced the 109s back to Croydon in what became a twenty-mile chase. Undeterred, Ferris managed

The Blohm & Voss Bv-142 was one of the few four-engine bomber designs the Germans tinkered with during the prewar and wartime era. Goering was an opponent of four-engine aircraft, and the idea of a strategic bomber never really took hold inside the Luftwaffe. The lack of such a weapon has often been used as a reason for the German failure during the Battle of Britain, but the truth is more nuanced than that.

A Ju-88 in flight. RAF pilots found the Ju-88 to be a very difficult opponent. Fast and decently armed, the Junkers rugged construction made it tough to bring down with the standard .303-caliber machine guns that armed the Spitfires and Hurricanes during the battle.

A Heinkel He-111 in flight. Capable of carrying over four thousand pounds of ordnance, the He-111 represented a marked improvement over the Dornier Do-17 and would eventually replace it as the backbone of the Luftwaffe's level bomber force.

to force-land, taxi to the dispersal area, and run to another Hurricane, where he fired up its Merlin engine and took off in hot pursuit of the Luftwaffe raid once again.

Meanwhile, 111 Squadron's second pass knocked down another Dornier 17. Only one German survived its comet-like plunge into the estuary. The others burned alive as their bombers became their fiery tombs.

Seventy-Four Squadron rolled into the action and tangled with part of the Bf-110 and Bf-109 escort. McCudden's old flight from 56 Squadron went after the Dorniers, but the German fighters held them at bay. One section from B Flight caught a 110 by surprise and knocked it out of the air.

A Heinkel 111 crew sits next to their bomber on an airfield in France, waiting the word to launch for the day's mission.

The He-111H was the most common Heinkel employed during the Battle of Britain. Some units added under wing bomb racks that allowed them to carry over six thousand pounds of bombs while maintaining a radius of action of over five hundred miles. In 1940, the He-111 was the closest the Luftwaffe had to a strategic bomber.

The Heinkel was originally designed as a civilian airliner that could quickly be converted to a bomber in order to get around the Versailles Treaty limitations that prohibited Germany from building an air force. In combat, the He-111 units flew in tight, mutually supportive formations that allowed them to mass what minimal air defense machine guns they possessed. *Apic/Getty Images*

The last seconds of a Ju-88.

Another Do-17 fell out of formation after Hurricanes raked its fuselage, killing one crew member and leaving two of remaining three badly wounded and bleeding at their stations. The desperate pilot fought to save his bomber and struggled to keep it aloft long enough to crash-land back in France.

In minutes, the raging fight ended and the gray, storm-filled skies over the estuary grew empty and silent. The RAF interceptors turned for home and set down at Manston and Croydon, two forward bases close to the Channel coast. At Croydon, 111 Squadron lost another Hurricane when Sgt. R. Carnall crashed on landing.

So began the first "official" day of the Battle of Britain. That night, the exhausted crews from KG-2 gathered for dinner and did their best not to notice the eleven empty seats around them. But the sight could not help but be a sobering one. The fighting would only escalate from there, and the German bomber unit had already lost 10 percent of its strength.

The British fared little better. Fighter Command started the Battle of Britain on a shoestring, without enough replacement pilots in the pipeline to keep pace with the losses the front-line units suffered. In 111 Squadron alone, the ensuing days of combat cost the unit most of its experienced pilots. Henry Ferris's fate symbolized the fate of so many of his flying comrades. On July 10, he set his battle damaged Hurri down back at Croydon, then charged back into the fight in a new mount. That aggressiveness defined most of the RAF fighter pilots that summer—they knew they were fighting for the fate of their nation—

Some of the few. In the summer of 1940, the fate of Great Britain—and the free world—rested on a couple hundred Hurricane and Spitfire pilots. They suffered appalling losses, but defeated the Luftwaffe in one of the most important campaigns of the twentieth century.

Two RAF pilots check out the ruins of a Heinkel He-111.

German Messerschmitt Bf-109 pilots lounge around at their flight line, waiting for news to scramble for the next mission.

yet it came at a very steep cost. Ferris died when he collided with a German bomber in another gut-check head-on pass a few weeks later.

The Battle of Britain became a titanic test of national will—just as Douhet envisioned. The winner would be the side that devoted the most resources to the fight and could survive the attrition rate among the clouds. The outcome of the battle ultimately determined the fate of Europe and much of the world, though the young fighter pilots defending England probably did not realize at the time how much the free world depended on their shoulders. Fifty-Six Squadron's commanding officer, G. A. L. "Minnie" Manton, later wrote:

> I don't think any of us really appreciated the seriousness of the situation. When we were scared to death five or six times a day, and yet find ourselves drinking in the local pub before closing time on a summer evening, it all seemed so unreal. . . .

If the British Hurricane and Spitfire pilots didn't see the big picture, the German high command completely stumbled on this front as well. For the first time, the Luftwaffe faced prosecuting

While Fighter Command bore the load of the Battle of Britain, RAF light and medium bombers struck at the seagoing invasion force the Germans assembled in French and Belgian coastal ports. Here, a Dutch RAF bomber crew makes some last-minute decisions prior to a mission's departure.

an air war without any other combined operations. There would be no panzers rolling for the enemy's capital, no Wehrmacht infantry infiltrating around frontier fortifications. For England to fall, the Luftwaffe would have to set the table alone.

And they blew it. In modern parlance, the Germans needed to execute a concentrated SEAD campaign. SEAD—suppression of enemy air defenses—in this case meant crushing or driving Fighter Command's squadrons away from the Channel coast. The Germans only needed to control the air from the French ports where the invasion barges were assembling to the beaches the Wehrmacht troops would storm in Southern England. That was the key to the entire battle, and the Germans—along with quite a few historians—missed it.

In fact, the Luftwaffe didn't even need to destroy all of Fighter Command. Divided into four parts—10 Group, 11 Group, 12 Group and 13 Group—only the first two were in the way of an invasion of Southern England. Twelve and 13 Groups covered north of London, the Midlands, and Scotland. While those squadrons could have been transferred down to 10 Group in Southern England or 11 Group in front of London, they would have done so only after the Luftwaffe had inflicted catastrophic casualties on the existing units in each command. Essentially, they would have rotated into the action just in time to be defeated in detail—if the Luftwaffe had focused its efforts on that one goal.

The Luftwaffe's short-ranged tactical aircraft could have achieved such a focused goal. Many postwar American and British historians have castigated the Germans for not having a four-engined long-range strategic bomber in their aerial arsenal. Blinded by their own nation's subsequent strategic campaign, they've missed the essential point: the air battle before the invasion was not in itself a strategic campaign, but a grand tactical one that required constant pressure on Fighter Command's airfields, command and control network, and the radar system that provided the British with such excellent ground control intercept capabilities.

Drug-addicted Hermann Goering visits his aviators. As the Battle of Britain wore on, he grew increasingly frustrated with his fighter pilots. They bore his wrath on many occasions and were forced to alter their tactics so drastically that eventually Goering all but chained them to the bombers during escort missions.

Werner Mölders rose to fame in 1940 as the commander of JG-51. During the Battle of France, he had been shot down, and while on his first flight during the Battle of Britain, he was wounded in a dogfight, possibly by RAF ace A. G. "Sailor" Malan.

Fighter Command had been organized around a series of fixed-sector station airfields that each included a couple of smaller satellite fields nearby. The satellite fields lacked the logistical and communication facilities of the sector stations. Destroying the sector stations—key installations like Biggin Hill, Kenley, Middle Wallop, and Hornchurch—would have played havoc not just with the many squadrons based there, but with Fighter Command's ability to react swiftly to any incoming raids.

Had this happened, the German air campaign would have set the strategic table for the next phase, the invasion of Southern England. It never came to that. Instead, the Germans squandered their massive numerical superiority by diffusing their effort on a variety of targets. The German objective for the air campaign was not the destruction of Fighter Command, it was the destruction of the entire Royal Air Force. As a result, Coastal Command and Bomber Command airfields were targeted throughout the summer, which in no way helped secure local air superiority over the Channel.

Additionally, the Luftwaffe planners chose to broaden the target spectrum to include aircraft and engine factories that supported the RAF. Other targets, such as docks, convoys, and naval bases were hit as well.

In fact, the Germans began the Battle of Britain almost half-heartedly. Hitler and much of his high command assumed that England would settle for peace after France fell. When that did not happen, the surprised Fuehrer gave the nod to the air campaign and the planned execution of the invasion.

Adolf Galland, left, commanded JG-26 during the 1940 campaign and rose to fame as one of Hitler's favorite fighter pilots. He would later become General of the Fighters and help organize the defense of the Reich against the USAAF Eighth and Fifteenth Air Force.

Confident and handsome, a well-heeled German bomber pilot named Captain Helbig. He poses with his Knight's Cross, one of the highest awards for valor in the air that the Luftwaffe could bestow.

Galland watches over a chess game between two of his aviators.

THE FIGHTERS

DURING THE BATTLE OF BRITAIN, the Germans learned the hard way that their bombers could not operate in hostile skies without strong fighter escort. Before the war, the Luftwaffe believed that high-speed medium bombers would be all but impervious to interception. The air campaigns against Poland and the West in 1940 seemed to support this conclusion. Then the Luftwaffe clashed head-on with the RAF, whose aircraft and pilots were their equals. Suddenly, the situation changed, and the outcome of the Battle of Britain depended on the ability of German fighter units to protect the bombers. An entire dynamic took shape, a battle within a battle, where the RAF tried different tactics to penetrate the escort shield, and the Germans developed countermeasures. Ultimately, Goering stepped in and ordered his fighter pilots to provide such close escort to the Heinkels and Junkers that they lost their freedom of movement and aggressiveness. Losses in the Bf-109 and Bf-110 units spiked as the British took advantage of this tactical shift. Instead of being relentlessly pursued all over the skies by the likes of Werner Mölders and Adolf Galland and their men, the British could now pick and choose their time to engage. Using speed and altitude, they could blow through the fighter escort, hit the bomber formation, and run to fight another day.

The key aircraft in this deadly subtext of the Battle of Britain were the Messerschmitt 109E, the Spitfire, and the Hurricane. All three became legendary aircraft of World War II. The Spitfire and the 109 saw combat from the first day of the war to the last, undergoing multiple upgrades and model developments during six years they served in front line units. The Hurricane, older and slower at the start of the war, gradually transitioned into a ground attack role. Equipped with 20mm cannon and sometimes even 40mm tank-busting Bofors, the Hurricane not only served as the backbone of Fighter Command in the summer of 1940, it gave the RAF its first truly effective ground attack aircraft. It saw service in all theaters until it was ultimately replaced by the Hawker Typhoon and Hawker Tempest in 1944.

The start of the battle in July reflected that reluctance. The Luftwaffe made tentative strikes against the coastal convoys, holding back its main strength in the process, instead of unleashing the full fury of the bomber and fighter geschwaders now arrayed against England in France and the Low Countries. Not only did this not serve any lasting purpose, it gave Fighter Command the chance to hone its interception techniques.

A month later, the Germans quit shadow boxing and threw the weight of their air force against England. August became the crucial month during the Battle of Britain as the Luftwaffe put such intense pressure on "the Few" that Fighter Command lost 26 percent of its fighter pilots. The Germans sporadically raided the sector airfields, doing telling damage at times. But again, they squandered the opportunity to simply focus on the air defense system and work its targets until it collapsed.

Despite their mistakes, the Germans had battered Fighter Command to the ropes. In the last ten days of August, the RAF lost 126 Hurricanes and Spitfires. So many experienced

Hitler decorates one of his Luftwaffe bomber commanders in 1940. As the Battle of Britain unfolded, the Fuehrer grew increasingly frustrated with the Luftwaffe's lack of apparent progress in destroying the RAF, and such medal ceremonies sometimes contained an underlying sense of tension since Hitler's displeasure with Goering and his aviators was well known. After Berlin was hit by the RAF in a night bombing raid in August, Hitler lost patience with the tactical campaign against the British and ordered the full scale terror bombing of London. That decision cost the Germans the Battle of Britain, and quite possibly, the war.

The Ju-88A had not arrived in large numbers by the time the Battle of Britain began. Had there been more available to the Luftwaffe, the campaign over Southern England might have gone differently. Able to hit targets in a traditional level bombing fashion, its ability to dive-bomb made it a superbly accurate weapon platform. It was used during the Battle of Britain not only as a harbinger of terror to the English people, but also to hit shipping in the Channel and bomb Fighter Command's airfields.

pilots had burned to death within those aircraft that Fighter Command was forced to pull raw replacements straight from operational training units and throw them into the battle. Other pilots were taken from Bomber and Coastal Commands and even the Fleet Air Arm, given minimal training, and sent into the air. They died at an appalling rate.

The mounting losses forced the British to change the way they intercepted incoming German raids. No longer could 11 Group risk pilots over the Channel, where if shot down

A Ju-88 crew, within the confined space of their plane's cockpit, flies toward England during a mission in 1940.

they had slender hopes of survival. Instead, they were ordered to break off pursuit of any German aircraft at the coastline. Nor would they attack German fighter formations any longer. Throughout August, whenever possible the British tried to hit the Messerschmitt escorts with their superior Spitfires, who would clear a path to the bombers for the slower but more rugged Hurricanes. Now, in growing desperation, 11 Group abandoned such balanced tactics and went all in for the bombers.

The Luftwaffe's units had suffered heavy losses as well, but their material superiority still gave them the edge. Plus, their fighter units had not been nearly as strained as the RAF's. Nevertheless, the British resistance began to have an effect on how the Nazi leadership perceived the battle. Impatient and frustrated, Hitler and his oddball minions could not understand why the Luftwaffe was taking so long to get the job done. After all, it took only forty days to conquer all of France. Poland fell in a few weeks.

Field Marshall Hermann Goering, the Luftwaffe commander, did not recognize the progress his air units had made against the RAF. Part of that was a result of bad intelligence,

but part of it was Goering's personality. The resolve of Fighter Command's increasingly inexperienced, young replacement pilots enraged "Fat Hermann." He demanded more and more of his units, excoriated his fighter pilots for perceived failures, and forced a change in escort tactics that tied the Bf-109s to the bomber formations so closely as to negate their freedom of movement.

To Hitler, Goering, and Field Marshall Albert Kesselring, it looked as if the attempt to destroy the Royal Air Force had failed. Right at the climactic moment, with Fighter Command almost driven to its knees, the Germans abandoned their attempt to achieve air superiority and totally lost sight of the purpose of the battle. Air superiority as a precursor to invasion was abandoned. From September 7 forward, the Luftwaffe would have one objective: terrorize the British populace into surrender.

On September 4, Hitler gave a speech in Berlin warning of the coming terror raids and declared "We will eradicate their cities!"

Three days later, the full might of the Luftwaffe was thrown directly at London's East End docks. The raid took on a vastly different character than previous Luftwaffe incursions. Instead of a number of small formations forming up over Calais and then heading to their different targets, some three hundred Heinkel He-111s, Dornier Do-17s, and Junkers Ju-88s climbed above 15,000 feet and swept toward London in a great phalanx. Almost six hundred Bf-109s and Bf-110s covered the aerial armada's flanks. The raiders made no feint or pretense: they headed straight for London.

A quiet, tranquil scene in a London park. Such afternoons became distant memories as the Luftwaffe poured its recourses into destroying the English capital.

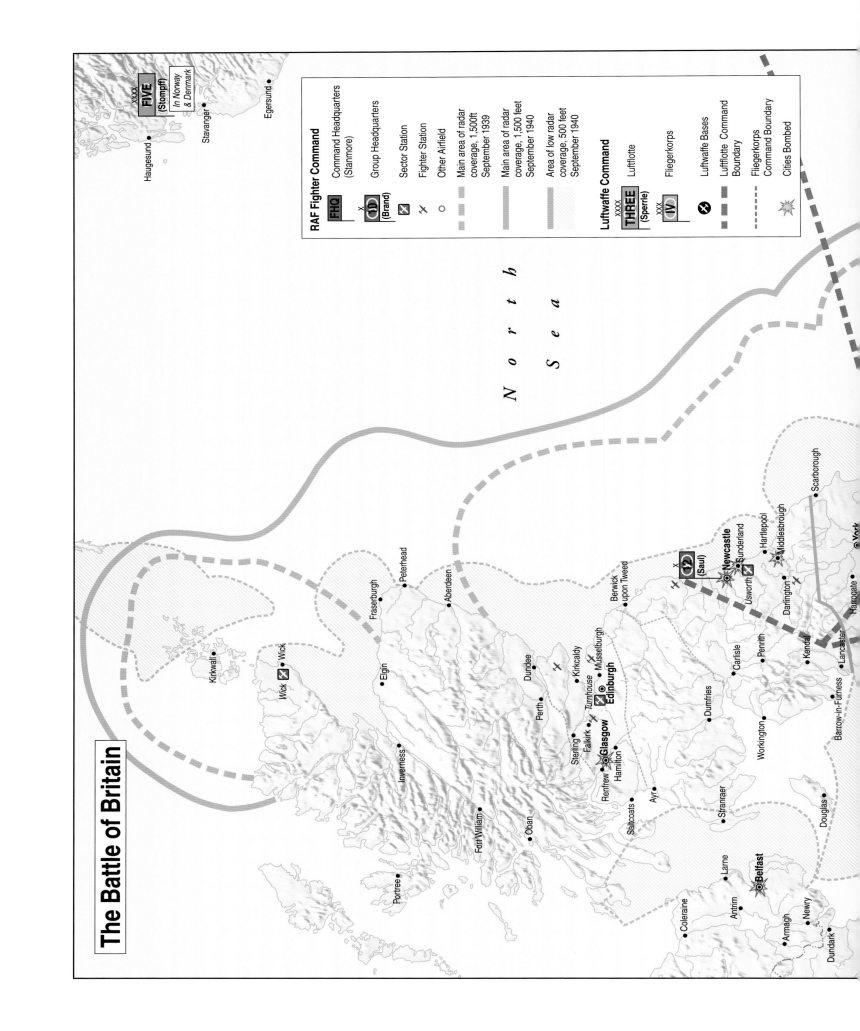

The Battle of Britain

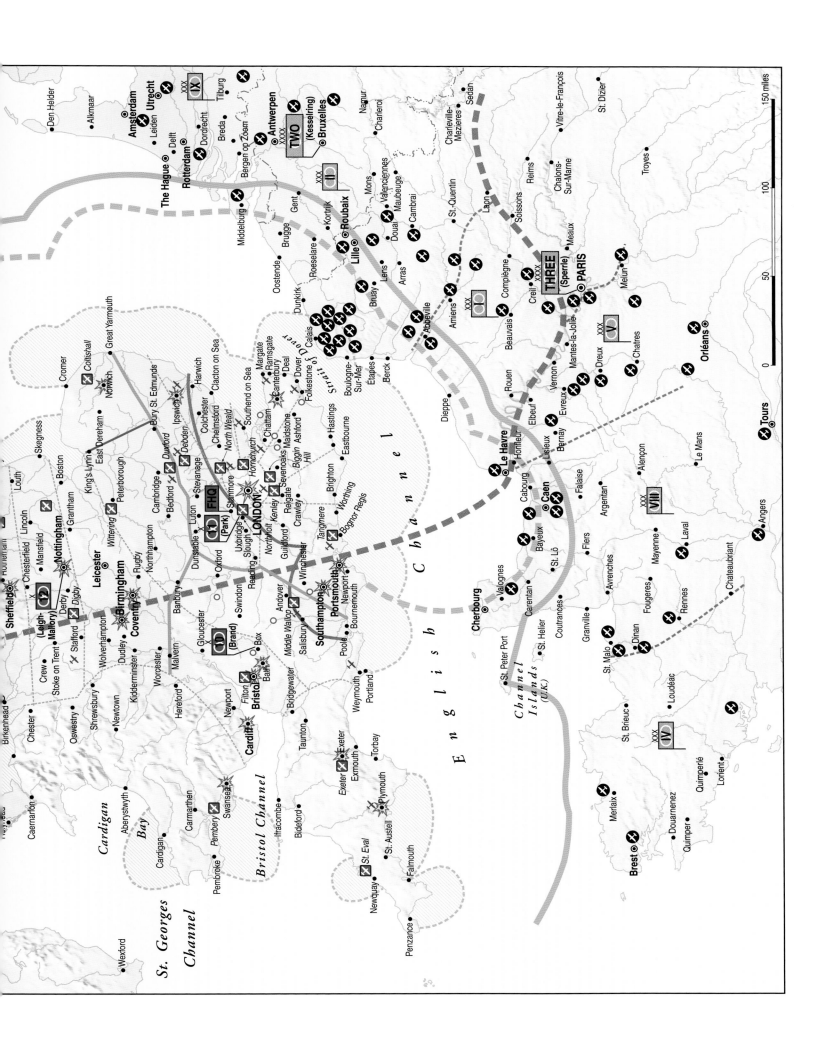

Eleven Group thought at first this was business as usual for the Luftwaffe. The British squadrons in front of London were scrambled to cover the sector stations and other high-value SEAD-related targets. As a result, the Germans had clear sky all the way to London. Only after most of the bombers dropped their payloads did the RAF manage to intercept the raid. The Polish volunteer pilots of 303 Squadron made a name for themselves that day when they ambushed a geschwader of about forty Do-17s, claiming about a quarter of the bombers for the loss of

The Blitz. In the second half of September, the Germans switched to night terror bombing to minimize their aircraft losses. The RAF had to scramble to meet that threat with new night interceptors.

Fire boats attempt to contain the damage to London's riverside warehouses and docks after the first major terror raid on the city in September 1940.

four of their Hurricanes. Altogether, the Germans suffered sixty-two aircraft damaged or destroyed. Forty-four Hurricanes or Spits were shot down or damaged as the fighting raged between London and the Channel.

London paid a heavy price as the air battle raged overhead. Bombs fell on the docks, warehouses, and factories along the East End, sparking massive conflagrations. At the West India Docks, a building loaded with rum took a bomb hit. Burning alcohol gushed from the warehouse, ignited everything in its path. In other places, the fires not only sent people fleeing for cover, but rats as well. In one notable instance, thousands of them swarmed out of a soap factory set ablaze during the bombing.

The human toll was extraordinary. Neighborhoods lay in ruins; houses burned and women, children, and men buried under piles of rubble struggled to survive. Rescue crews began digging them out even as thousands of firefighters converged on the area to fight the flames. The first raid ended at six that evening, but 250 more bombers arrived at supper time to deliver another hammer-blow to the East Side. Silverton, an industrial section of the city surrounded by neighborhoods of small houses built in the mid-nineteenth century, erupted in flames. The bombs cut swaths right through the old houses, blowing civilians to bits and leaving the survivors gasping in horror at the human carnage.

Ever after, Londoners called September 7 "Black Saturday."

Day after day, the Luftwaffe returned to sow more destruction on the English capital. Thousands of civilians died in the attacks, but British morale did not break. The Germans had failed to learn a vital lesson from Poland and Holland: terror bombing as an instrument of political power only worked if the enemy government saw no remaining hope or options left to continue the fighting. In the Polish example, Warsaw had been surrounded and its water supply compromised. They could not have held out much longer, and the terror raids merely hastened the Polish surrender, not caused it. Same thing happened in Holland. The Dutch government knew it could not defend the civilian populace any longer and did the humanitarian thing in an attempt to save lives.

Britain did not face the same desperate situation in September 1940. The Germans still had to get across the

While the Spitfire equipped only a limited number of Fighter Command's squadrons at the start of the Battle of Britain, it was the RAF's most formidable point defense fighter and interceptor. Its remarkable performance made it more than a match for a Messerschmitt 109. One RAF tactic was to use a Spitfire squadron to distract a Luftwaffe raid's fighter escort. While engaged with the Spitfires, Hurricanes would use the chance to attack the Luftwaffe's bombers.

The human effect of terror bombing. Hundreds of Londoners take refuge in the subway system. In the years that followed this scene, the people of Germany would experience this tenfold.

A tight formation of He-111s en route to their target. The Battle of Britain became the first pure air campaign in history, and it went a long way to discrediting the prewar theorists like Douhet, who believed that airpower alone would break an enemy population to its knees.

After the experience of the Battle of Britain, the RAF realized the shortcomings of the .303-caliber machine gun that equipped the Hurricanes and Spitfires. Later versions of the Hurricane, like these, carried four 20mm cannons that were far more deadly against German bombers than the older small-caliber machine guns.

Channel. Every day, the citizens of London could look skyward and see the interleaved contrails that told them Fighter Command was still fighting ferociously for them. Falling bombers landed in farmer's fields, where the crews were captured by the local civilians. Other German aircraft crashed in London itself, or the surrounding towns. The British population knew they were not helpless to the onslaught, and that played a major role in maintaining civilian morale.

Worse, for the Germans, the switch to terror bombing gave Fighter Command the respite it needed to survive and continue to intercept raids effectively. The number of attacks on the sector stations and satellite fields dropped off, giving base personnel time to repair damage both to their facilities and to the Hurricanes and Spitfires so badly needed in the air.

For the rest of the month, losses staggered both sides. Fighter Command lost 28 percent of its fighter pilots in those crucial thirty days. The Messerschmitt units suffered a staggering 23 percent loss rate. The number of empty chairs in the mess halls grew as the month wore on. On September 15, now known as "Battle of Britain Day" in the United Kingdom, the fighting reached its zenith. Exhausted Luftwaffe survivors of the summer's fighting climbed into their cockpits, manned their machine gun positions aboard their bombers and sped back into the fight. Bone weary British fighter pilots who had flown to the edge of their physical and mental endurance for weeks now, lay in the grass near their aircraft, waiting with dread for the phone call and summons, "Full squadron scramble!" that would send them into the fray once again. For the remaining Few, the operational tempo in September had become a marathon test of human endurance. Four, five, and sometimes six intercept missions a day became the norm. And on every return to their home field, fewer men were left to lounge in the summer's grass in the shadow of their bullet-scarred fighters.

By the end of September 15, the BBC announced the destruction of 185 German planes. The true figure unearthed after the war was 79 destroyed or damaged, but that in no way diminished the magnitude of the day's victory for the RAF. After the fifteenth, the raids gradually slacked off and the Germans switched to bombing under the cover of darkness. The Blitz grew into a nightly ordeal for the citizens of London. Thousands more perished in the flames and rubble. October and November saw massive raids shatter entire districts. On November 14, in Operation Moonlight Sonata, five hundred Heinkels, Dorniers, and Junkers carpet bombed the city of Coventry. The flames and high-explosive ordnance destroyed over four thousand houses and burned out 75 percent of the city's factories. At least six hundred civilians died, including a large number of firefighters killed when their headquarters took a bomb hit.

Morale never wavered. Britain did not submit to terror. Guilio Douhet's nihilistic vision of future warfare, once put to the ultimate test, proved bankrupt. The Germans gave up on the invasion of England, and when the terror bombing failed to break the British people, Hitler essentially lost interest in the campaign. He turned his attention to Russia and all the twisted plans Nazi ideology had laid for the Slavic people in Eastern Europe. If he could not destroy Britain, he'd at least neutralized them as a threat, or so Hitler thought. This would give Germany the time needed to knock out Soviet Russia and create a Nazi agrarian paradise in its place, all the while plundering the conquered lands for all their natural resources.

While the Messerschmitt Bf-110 failed as a daylight fighter, it gained a new lease on life as a bomb-carrying, fast fighter-bomber. Hard to catch due to its swiftness, the Luftwaffe used the 110 to strike at a variety of targets, including shipping and RAF airfields. Here, a BF-110 releases its bombs on a British merchant vessel.

A JG-26 Bf-109E. The Luftwaffe fighter pilots wanted to have the freedom of movement needed to roam the flanks of the bomber formations in search of RAF fighters to attack. Such loose escort tactics enraged Goering, who ordered his 109 pilots to fly virtually wing-to-wing with the bombers they were assigned as escort. Thus hobbled, the 109s could not seize the initiative and drive the RAF out of the air. In fact, the 109s became easy targets by marauding British fighters.

The Bf-109E's cockpit layout.

A. G. "Sailor" Malan became one of the great RAF fighter leaders of the Battle of Britain. Reported to have shot down German ace Werner Mölders, Malan commanded the legendary 74 Squadron during the summer of 1940. A South African by birth, Malan eventually was credited with twenty-seven aerial kills. It was men like Sailor Malan who ensured Britain's survival and delivered a resounding defeat to the vaunted Luftwaffe.

Britain did indeed have very little offensive capability with which to strike back at Germany in late 1940. The army was still re-equipping after its defeat in France and would not be ready to return to the Continent for years. The Royal Navy, as Churchill put it, could lose the war but could not win it. Embroiled in the war against the U-boats and the fighting in the Mediterranean, the Royal Navy had been stretched to the limit, much like Fighter Command had been in August.

Churchill cast about for any weapon with which to wield offensively against Germany. He concluded there was only one: Bomber Command.

The Bristol Beaufighter arrived in the nick of time for the RAF. With a reasonable top speed, heavy armament, and good range, the Beau served as a multirole fighter-bomber and night fighter. In the latter role, the Beaufighter functioned as both an interceptor of German nocturnal raiders as well as an escort for Bomber Command's missions over Western Europe.

4

RESPONSE IN KIND

★ ★ ★ ★ ★

They told me when they cut the ready wheat,
The hares are suddenly homeless and afraid,
And aimlessly sicle the stubble with scared feet,
Finding no place in sunlight or shade.

It's morning and the Hampdens have returned.
The crews are home, have stretched and laughed and gone,
Whence the planes came and the Chance-light burned
The sun has ridden the sky and made the dawn.

He walks distraught, circling the landing ground,
Waiting the last one home that won't come back,
And like those hares, he wanders round and round,
Lost and desolate on the close cropped track.
—"Missing," by Herbert Corby

At the start of the war, the RAF lacked a truly effective long-range strategic bomber. The Bristol Blenheim was among the mediocre twin-engine designs that formed the backbone of Britain's offensive aviation.

EVEN AS FIGHTER COMMAND FOUGHT to protect the skies over Southern England, Bomber Command took the first baby steps forward to bring the war home to the German people. The counteroffensive—in the best Douhet fashion—started with a whimper instead of a bang, mainly as a result of a complete lack realistic prewar preparation for the mechanics of bombing cities hundreds of miles from England.

In mid-1940, Bomber Command was a flat-out mess. Its squadrons lacked everything from decent aircraft to effective navigational aids and useful payload capacities. The crews were green as grass, and every time they'd been thrown into the fray, bad things happened. The first days of the war proved that when the RAF sent its first raids against German naval targets, it lost most of the aircraft dispatched.

During the Battle of France, the light bomber squadrons sent to try and blunt the panzer penetrations in Holland and Belgium ran into a firestorm of flak and Bf-109s. Flying fossilized aircraft like the virtually defenseless Fairey Battle, these brave crews died in droves to no strategic purpose.

As the Battle of Britain unfolded, Bomber Command's best aircraft was the Vickers Wellington. Twin-engined, fabric-covering its rugged geodetic frame, the "Wimpy," as the crews affectionately called it, could carry 4,500 pounds of bombs to targets almost a thousand miles away. Armed with only six .303-caliber light machine guns, the Wellington could hardly defend itself against determined daylight interceptors, a fact the Luftwaffe drove home repeatedly in 1939. In December of that year, three Wellington squadrons attempted to bomb Schillig Roads and Wilhelmshaven, only to lose ten Wimpys, with another three badly damaged. After that, Bomber Command abandoned long-range unescorted daylight raids against Germany. Such missions just proved too costly with the aircraft available, and the RAF could not maintain the loss rate of crews and bombers.

Initially, the RAF's ability to strike back at Germany was limited not only by the aircraft in its inventory, but by the technology required to get its bombers to their target areas at night. The RAF had trained throughout the 1930s as a daylight bombing force. When the first Blenheim and Wellington raids resulted in unsustainable losses, night bombing looked to be the only way for Britain to strike back at Germany. Much would have to be learned and developed on the job. In the meantime, the aircrews paid for that process with their lives.

The Vickers Wellington was the closest thing to a heavy strategic bomber the RAF could field at the outset of the war. It would dominate Bomber Command's squadrons for almost the first three years of the war.

With its rugged construction, reliable engines and ability to carry a good payload, the Wellington was the indispensable weapon of the nocturnal air war. Yet, when used in daylight operations, their light defensive armament made them easy prey for Axis interceptors.

A 1,000-pound bomb about to be loaded aboard a Wellington. The British developed a whole range of specialized ordnance designed to maximize the destruction wrought on German cities. From incendiaries to start fires to "blockbuster" bombs intended to destroy water, sewer, and gas mains, the RAF became the leading agent of urban devastation.

Besides the Wellington, Bomber Command fielded a motley collection of mediocre early 1930s designs, such as the Armstrong-Whitworth Whitley and the Handley Page Hampden. In 1936, the RAF asked the British aircraft industry to build a true long-range strategic bomber. The Short Stirling and the Avro Manchester resulted from that process, but four years later neither had yet reached operational status. Bad luck and poor design decisions hampered the development of both bombers. The Stirling prototype crashed during its maiden flight in 1939, underscoring multiple issues that took many months to sort out. The Manchester didn't have much more success. Equipped with four engines powering two propellers, the aircraft had a distressing habit of spontaneously combusting while in flight.

The missions flown against Germany in 1940 highlighted the problems of nocturnal long-range bombing. First, navigation played a vital factor in the success of any raid. Throughout the fall, a large proportion of crews could not locate their targets in the dark. Given how few aircraft were available for offensive operations in 1940, every bomber that failed to find its way in the dark whittled down Bomber Command's ability to do serious harm to the Germans. Not that much harm was being done by those aircraft that found their targets. Post-strike reconnaissance photos showed that few bombs fell within a mile of where they were intended. Such accuracy did not lend itself to surgical, precision strikes.

Another case study in mediocrity: the Armstrong-Whitworth Whitley equipped many Bomber Command squadrons at the start of the war. Totally inadequate for the strategic campaign against Germany, the shortage of modern bombers forced it to remain in service well past its prime.

The Messerschmitt Bf-110 came into its own as a night interceptor. Equipped with two 20mm cannons mounted in the fuselage behind the pilot and set to fire upward at a forty-five degree angle, the 110 crews would attack British bombers from their vulnerable bellies. The Bf-110 also carried an airborne radar system that could help the pilot hone in on a target after being guided to the stream by ground controllers. The Luftwaffe's night fighter force remained a deadly effective threat until late 1944.

What to do about these issues? That question plagued Bomber Command through 1942 as it struggled to re-equip and train for the task at hand. But in 1940, the British bomber crews lived in the shadow of their own technological and material shortcomings. Not much could be accomplished in that environment, except to lay the foundation for future operations through hard-won experience and the blood of the young crews.

There would be hope and successes in the future, but in 1940 the pipeline looked pretty empty. Bomber Command settled into its role with the aircraft it went to war with in 1939, which meant the young men sent aloft night after night paid the price for the prewar neglect. Nevertheless, Churchill was right: Bomber Command served as the only way Britain could wield offensive action against Germany in 1940. Its army could never face the Wehrmacht alone; the navy could win the Battle of the Atlantic and secure the Mediterranean, but its ships could not defeat Germany.

As a result, Churchill and most of his senior military advisors agreed that Bomber Command gave the country the best chance of ultimate victory. In October 1940, Chief

One of Bomber Command's more numerous medium bombers at the start of the war, the Handley Page Hampden was such an ergonomic nightmare that its crews called it the "Flying Suitcase." Shoehorned into tight confines within its narrow fuselage, the RAF airmen could drag aloft four thousands pounds of bombs over a radius of action of about five hundred miles. Armed with only four (later six) popgun .303-caliber machine guns, it was meat on the table for Luftwaffe interceptors when used in daylight. Out of necessity, the Hampden soldiered on until late 1942. By the time they were withdrawn from front-line service, half had been lost in operational accidents or in combat over the Third Reich.

A Bomber Command crew mounts up at sunset. Though Douhet and other theorists believed a strategic bombing campaign could bring about a cheap victory, the reality turned out to be vastly different. This young RAF crew had about a 75 percent chance of dying, being wounded, or falling into German hands.

The Avro Manchester offered a glimmer of hope that Bomber Command might receive new first-rate long-range aircraft with which to pummel Germany. Powered by four engines linked to a pair of propellers, the Manchester never met expectations. Fussy, complex, and prone to fatal engine fires, the Manchester equipped only a tiny number of Bomber Command squadrons. Its greatest contribution to the war effort was to serve as the first design stepping stone to the much more successful Lancaster.

The Blackburn Botha represented one of the worst design failures that plagued the British aircraft industry in the late 1930s. Intended to be a four-seat reconnaissance aircraft and torpedo bomber, the Botha was dangerously underpowered and difficult to fly. It proved to be unsuitable for front-line operations and was relegated to anti-submarine patrol work until replaced by other, more successful aircraft.

When the Blenheim, Hampden, and Wellingtons sent over Germany in 1939 ended up getting shot down in droves by the Luftwaffe's air defenses, the British Air Ministry went searching for a new medium bomber that could survive such daylight operations. The Bristol Buckingham was the product of that search. It took two years to get the Buckingham in the air, and despite its top speed of over three hundred miles per hour, the RAF no longer really needed a daylight medium bomber. It represented another diversion of effort and resources at a time when Bomber Command was struggling desperately to expand in the face of production issues and incredibly high losses.

of the Air Staff Sir Charles Portal sent Bomber Command a directive that essentially served as a blueprint for its operations for the remainder of the war. There would be two top priority targets: German morale and Germany's oil industry. British air planners studied Nazi Germany's wartime economy and concluded the weak link was its oil infrastructure. Should the synthetic fuel refineries be destroyed, the panzers could not roll. The Heinkels could not fly.

The British would fight fire with fire. The London Blitz and all the devastation the Germans had wrought on the Kingdom's capital had removed whatever moral qualms the British leadership had at pursuing the destruction of Germany's cities and killing its civilian populace. The gloves came off that October, and in the years to come, the German people would feel the wrath for Warsaw, Rotterdam, and London a hundredfold. Douhet's cold vision of future air warfare would become Germany's reality for five long years.

Nevertheless, there were problems with assaulting morale by killing civilians. First, the British looked back in time and saw how the German home front collapsed in 1918 and concluded that Germany's people would not be able to put up with the hardship of area attacks on their cities. The British made the same mistake Goering and Hitler made in September 1940 and completely underestimated the resolve of those upon which the bombs fell. National morale, never an easy thing to gauge in the first place, served as an elusive objective, a will-of-the-wisp sort of target that could be chased but never really seized. In 1940, however, this was unclear, and the men making the decisions believed pounding German cities to rubble would cause systemic collapse and the end to World War II.

The oil industry, on the other hand, formed the weak link in Germany's war machine, and no doubt its facilities were legitimate military targets with no moral ambiguity surrounding their destruction. Unfortunately for the British, these targets tended to be isolated, away from cities and small enough to defy even the best bombing accuracy the RAF crews could offer early in the war. Additionally, most of the major oil facilities, such as Ploesti, lay in Eastern Europe and were either out of range to Bomber Command's early war aircraft or left the crews dangerously exposed to interception for lengthy periods of time. As a result, the targets in 1940 and 1941 tended to be "industrial centers"—cities with lots of factories where falling bombs were likely to do some damage no matter how far off the intended mark they landed.

Through November and December 1940, Bomber Command embarked on its new, well-defined campaign. Five raids were launched against Berlin, three more against Hamburg. All eight combined managed to put fewer than six hundred individual sorties over Germany, resulting in little damage and quite a few RAF losses. After one particularly rough night in which Bomber Command lost eleven planes, Churchill personally despaired over such casualties and made it clear to the RAF's leadership that they could not be sustained.

In 1941, the first of the four-engined bombers finally reached operational status. The Short Stirling finally flew its first combat mission in February 1941. Ironically, Bomber Command sent these new aircraft against Rotterdam. Throughout the year, Stirlings arrived in dribs and drabs, but there were never enough to equip more than a couple of squadrons. Same with the Manchesters, whose operational record did not merit the effort and treasure devoted to the project.

Fortunately, in March 1941, the first Handley Page Halifax squadron flew a mission against German naval targets at Le Havre, France. Over seven years in development, the Halifax represented the first effective four-engined bomber to achieve operational status in Europe. Capable of carrying an astonishing 13,500-pound bomb load over seven hundred miles to its target and back, the Halifax gave the RAF its first aerial sledgehammer with which to batter Germany's cities. The problem was that there weren't enough of them to make a difference. Throughout the year, Bomber Command averaged only twenty-three operational Halifaxes between two squadrons. Teething troubles and technical bugs kept the serviceability rates down.

In desperation, the British turned to the United States for help and purchased a squadron's worth of Boeing B-17Cs. Dubbed the Fortress I, these rugged, long-legged bombers gave the RAF high hopes. Once operational with 90 Squadron, a whole array of problems cropped up with them. First, the manually operated defensive guns turned out to be almost useless in battle. The fuselage blisters had to be opened in order to use those guns, which

The Short Stirling was the first long-ranged four engine aircraft to join Bomber Command. Entering service in 1941, its pilots discovered that at altitude, the Stirling could actually outmaneuver Ju-88 and Bf-110 interceptors, something the later Halifax and Lancaster could not do.

A formation of Hampden bombers over England. The crews of this poorly defended medium bomber faced long odds of survival over Germany.

The demand for offensive aircraft was so great that the RAF ordered hundreds of Lockheed Hudsons to fill the gap the British aviation industry could not close. Used in reconnaissance, light bomber, and anti-submarine warfare roles, the Hudson gave good service through the early years of the war.

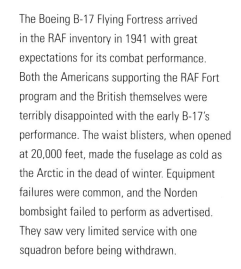

The Boeing B-17 Flying Fortress arrived in the RAF inventory in 1941 with great expectations for its combat performance. Both the Americans supporting the RAF Fort program and the British themselves were terribly disappointed with the early B-17's performance. The waist blisters, when opened at 20,000 feet, made the fuselage as cold as the Arctic in the dead of winter. Equipment failures were common, and the Norden bombsight failed to perform as advertised. They saw very limited service with one squadron before being withdrawn.

exposed the crew to freezing cold temperatures at high altitude. The Fortress I also lacked armor protection. Disappointed, 90 Squadron flew only fifty-one sorties before handing their Forts over to Coastal Command in September 1941. On one mission to Bremen, not a single Boeing even hit the city during their high-altitude bomb runs.

On the night of November 7–8, 1941, Bomber Command launched four hundred aircraft against targets all over Europe. The crews flew missions to mine Oslo harbor in Norway and bomb Berlin and other cities in Germany. Thirty-seven bombers and 120 airmen went down that night, victims of anti-aircraft fire and the Luftwaffe's growing night fighter capabilities. In Berlin, the attack wrecked 390 homes and killed nine civilians.

Wellingtons not only served in Bomber Command, but also functioned as anti-submarine patrol aircraft as well as search and rescue birds.

In the early years of the war, the RAF's near-single-minded focus on the strategic air war against Germany and the industrial build-up required to support it came at the expense of the daylight, tactical level-bombing capabilities. The British purchased the North American B-25 Mitchell to help fill this need.

The initial expansion of Bomber Command was hampered by delayed design development, production problems, and the failure of some key projects, including the Avro Manchester. In the 1930s, the British aviation industry struggled to bring to production an entire crop of new bombers, such as the Short Stirling, which took five years to go from concept to combat operational. As these growing pains hampered the expansion of the force, the older designs, such as these Blenheims, were forced to remain in front-line service long after they had become obsolete.

For a year, a patchwork force of obsolescent medium bombers carried the fight to Germany's cities with very little results for the effort. As the campaign continued, it became clear that better aircraft and better equipment would be needed to inflict substantial damage on targets in the Third Reich. The first glimmer of hope arrived on the wings of the outstanding Handley Page Halifax, a powerful and effective four-engine bomber that reached operational status in March 1941. Available in very limited numbers through that year, the Halifax eventually became the second-most numerous aircraft in Bomber Command's arsenal behind the Avro Lancaster.

The Consolidated Liberator ended up being one of the most successful of the Lend-Lease bombers employed by the RAF. Used both as a bomber as well as an anti-submarine patrol aircraft with Coastal Command, the Liberator's heavy ordnance load and long range played a valuable role in operations in Europe and the Mediterranean.

The early export variant of the B-24 was called the Consolidated LB-30. Lacking power turrets and many of the features found on the later B-24D model, the LB-30 saw limited service. Many were later converted into transports.

The night spelled utter disaster for the British. The nation had pinned its hopes on Douhet's theories and had undertaken a massive effort to expand bomber command so that it would ultimately field a force of some four thousand aircraft. Yet, the expansion had gone slowly, and what raids reached their targets had yet to inspire much hope that serious damage could be inflicted. A change was needed. A few months later, in February 1942, Sir Arthur Harris was appointed the new chief of Bomber Command. Single-minded, directed, and

Striking back. In 1940, the British had no other way to launch a counteroffensive against Germany besides Bomber Command's aircraft and crews. Sir Charles Portal, Chief of the Air Staff, sent a directive to the RAF that October that laid the foundations for the British strategic bombing campaign for the next five years. German morale would be the primary target, and destroying the Third Reich's cities would be the means to strike at it. Killing civilians had become official British policy.

Bombing up a Wellington the afternoon before a night mission. Until the arrival of the Halifax and the Lancaster, the Wellington remained the most versatile and effective bomber in the RAF's inventory.

energetic, Harris believed wholeheartedly in the concept of area bombing. In the months to come, he would reshape Bomber Command from the struggling, fledgling force it was into a formidable weapon that could lay waste to entire cities. He did it with such ruthlessness of purpose that his own men, upon whose shoulders the campaign depended, sometimes called him "Butcher Harris," especially on those mornings when dozens of bombers failed to return home from the dark skies over Nazi Germany.

Nevertheless, the stage was set. Bomber Command had a new leader. New weapons, including the deadly 4,000-pound "blockbuster" bomb, had been perfected. New tactics, new countermeasures, and new aircraft would soon reach operational status. As they did, Germany's population would be in the crosshairs in what became the largest air war in human history.

The USAAF banked on the B-17 Flying Fortress and its crews to deliver the knockout blows against the Third Reich. The United States invested considerable resources, money, and manpower on the creation of a strategic bombing force shaped by the B-17's exceptional capabilities and defensive armament.

5

THE AMERICANS ARRIVE

THEY CAME TO THE WAR AS FLEDGLINGS, high of spirit, confident in their aircraft, and wed to the concept of daylight precision bombing. In February 1942, just as Sir Arthur Harris took over Bomber Command, the advance wave of what would become a flood of hundreds of thousands of officers and airmen arrived in England from the United States. The Americans had arrived.

That advanced echelon included the commander of the recently activated Eighth Air Force, Maj. Gen. Carl Spaatz. A Mitchellite to the core, Spaatz appeared at Bomber Command's headquarters at High Wycombe on February 23, 1942. He and Harris hit it off at once. They were kindred souls with unshakable faith in the ability of airpower to win the war, though they differed in the details. Thanks to the RAF's earlier hard knocks, Bomber Command would stick to night attacks for the majority of the war. Spaatz believed that the latest-generation B-17 had all the defensive armament needed to conduct long-range missions in the teeth of Luftwaffe fighter interception. If flown in close, mutually protective formations, a B-17 group could field all-round defense with literally hundreds of deadly .50-caliber machine guns.

Through the spring, aircraft and men trickled in from the United States. It was not an impressive force at first, and on the streets of London there was much gossip about the big-talking Americans who had yet to actually measure up to their own words.

The measuring up would take time. First, the USAAF had to learn hard lessons of its own.

On Independence Day 1942, six American crews from the 15th Bomb Group (Light) climbed into aircraft borrowed from their RAF mentors in 226 Squadron. Ironically, 226 flew Douglas

The Americans joined the fight in the 1942, full of confidence in the Boeing B-17 Flying Fortress. The RAF's lessons with the early variants of the B-17 led to significant refinements that Boeing incorporated into the E model. This was not the same Fort that failed so grievously with 90 Squadron, RAF the previous year, and the E model laid the groundwork for the USAAF's bombing campaign in Europe.

The Americans entered the European Air War on the Fourth of July 1942. Using borrowed Lend-Lease Douglas Boston bombers, a small USAAF contingent took part in a low-altitude raid on German targets in Holland. From this tiny step would spring forth thousand-plane raids that tore the industrial heart out of the Third Reich only two years later.

DB-7 "Boston" bombers, the Lend-Lease version of the venerable A-20 Havoc. For one mission, those aircraft were loaned back to the native sons of the country that provided the RAF with these excellent aerial weapons.

The Americans formed half the strike formation that day. Four Vs of three Bostons each sped low over the North Sea to target German airfields in Holland. By staying low, they sought to avoid radar detection, but Axis vessels steaming through the area spoiled their element of surprise by reporting the incoming raid.

Once the Bostons reached the Dutch coast, the formation split up and raced for their airfield targets. The Allied force flew straight into ferocious and accurate anti-aircraft fire. The

Carl Spaatz awards the Distinguished Service Cross to Maj. Charles Kegelman for his personal courage and flying skills during the USAAF's first raid on German targets in Northwest Europe.

Germans spared nothing when it came to airfield defense, and attacking such targets remained one of the most difficult and costly missions of the air war for low-flying tactical aircraft and fighter-bombers.

The Allies paid a heavy price that Fourth of July. Two of the six American crews went down in flames. A third USAAF-manned Boston took a flak hit in the engine and scraped the ground while streaking across De Kooy Airdrome. Flames feathering back from the stricken fan, the Boston pilot somehow managed to pull up and get his crew home safely, a feat that earned him a Distinguished Service Cross, the second-highest award for valor next to the Congressional Medal of Honor.

The British also lost a Boston on the mission, making this first American foray against the Germans a costly one indeed. A fourth of the bomber force succumbed to flak. It was a taste of things to come.

That summer, the first of the heavy bomb groups arrived in Great Britain. The 97th earned that honor, setting up operations at RAF Polebrook. Flying the new B-17E, the 97th lacked training, experience and tactical knowledge. Some of the navigators didn't know how to navigate. Some of the radio operators couldn't even read or send Morse code. Few of the men had ever conducted flights over 20,000 feet. In fact, most had never even strapped on their oxygen masks.

And yet, the 97th would serve as the seed unit for what would become the most massive air effort ever put forth by the United States. Everything has a start point, no matter how

Another photo of RAF Bostons during a raid on a French port.

successful or not. For the Mighty Eighth, it began on August 17, 1942, when the 97th carried out a twelve-plane raid against a railroad marshalling yard at Rouen, France. Over a hundred Royal Air Force Spitfires provided heavy escort force for the bombers. Experience had shown the Luftwaffe's fighter units in France, which included the elite Jagdgeschwader 26, could be deadly effective adversaries in their new Focke-Wulf 190 "Butcher Birds."

Flying in a B-17 named *Yankee Doodle* on that first mission was Gen. Ira Eaker, head of VIII Bomber Command. He'd come along to see for himself how the 97th would fare. The co-pilot of *Butcher Bird*, the lead aircraft that day was Maj. Paul Tibbets. In 1945, Tibbets would pilot the *Enola Gay* over Hiroshima and his crew would drop the first atomic bomb used in battle.

The raid succeeded beyond all expectations. The dozen Forts dropped almost 40,000 pounds of British-built bombs on the target area. Post-strike reconnaissance showed an impressive, tight pattern to the destruction wrought on the ground. The Norden bombsight

appeared to be a wonder device after all. Nothing the British could do at night matched this level of accuracy.

What's more, not a single B-17 went down. All the crews returned safely to England, and there was much revelry that evening at Polebrook. There wouldn't be many good days ahead like this one. In fact, two missions later, a Messerschmitt made a pass at Tibbetts' B-17. A 20 mm cannon shell exploded in the cockpit, which wounded him with shrapnel and nearly took his co-pilot's left hand off.

Still, the Rouen raid served as a good beginning for the nascent Eighth Air Force. It also made excellent propaganda and quieted the British down for awhile. To counter that English attitude, Spaatz took to carrying recon photos of strike damage in his pocket. He'd pull them out and show the results of precision bombing to anyone who wanted to take a look.

Elated at the results, Spaatz and Eaker set about laying the foundations for the massive force they hoped to field against Germany. Through the summer and fall, new bomb groups

Later in August, the Eighth Air Force flew its first combat mission. Flying B-17Es, the 97th Bomb Group struck rail targets at Rouen, France, without loss. It was an auspicious beginning to what would become one of the longest attritional campaigns in U.S. history. Here, a squadron of B-17s forms up over England in preparation for a mission in 1942.

The Eighth Air Force had to develop tactics, formations, and procedures almost from scratch when its crews began flying missions in 1942. Combat experience honed and refined those tactics and techniques and led to innovations from the squadron level on up.

General Ira Eaker commanded VIII Bomber Command, then later the Eighth Air Force during its formative stages through the end of the brutal 1943 campaign.

reached England, including the 303rd and 93rd. The 1st Fighter Group and its P-38s flew across the Atlantic to join VIII Fighter Command. In time, the 31st, 52nd, and 4th Fighter Groups would form the initial core of the available escort force.

Through the rest of the fall, the Eighth Air Force devoted most of its energy against U-boat targets in support of the campaign in the North Atlantic. These deeply unpopular missions contributed little to the Allied cause. By this time, the U-boat pens in the French ports like St. Nazaire had been reinforced with a twenty foot concrete roof. The bombs the B-17s did get on these targets exploded harmlessly on the surface of these massive structures. Worse, the missions exposed the B-17 crews to heavy fighter and anti-aircraft attack. For the men who laid their lives on the line daily to carry out these sorties, such a ridiculous target selection frustrated and demoralized them.

Meanwhile, the build up gained steam until Operation Torch derailed everything. This was the invasion of Northwest Africa by a combined Anglo-American force. To carry out this operation, the Allies needed every available plane to support it. The Eighth was stripped of most of its fighter units, including the 1st, 31st, and 52nd groups, and lost some of its B-17 outfits as well. Spaatz and Eaker protested to no avail. Eventually, the Eighth lost 1,250 aircraft and 30,000 men. The bombing campaign came to a crashing halt. In December, the Eighth lost its talented commander, General Spaatz to the Mediterranean theater as well. Ira Eaker took his place It would not be until the following January that the fledglings in England would commence large-scale bombing operations against Nazi-held Europe.

As the Americans arrived in England, then had their build-up derailed by Torch, Bomber Command's night raids began to cause substantial damage. Soon after taking over, Harris wanted to make a statement, both to the British people and to Germany, by launching the RAF's first

Through the 1930s, the standard USAAF bomber formation remained the elongated V. In Europe, the Fort crews realized that such an arrangement did not maximize the firepower their aircraft carried. The bomb groups began to experiment with new formations designed to give the Fort gunners overlapping fields of fire. The combat box emerged from this formative period and was widely adopted throughout the Eighth in short order.

B-17Es on a training bomb run back in the States. As the air war over Europe developed into a titanic struggle of attrition, rapid and effective crew training became one of the most important logistical elements in defeating the Luftwaffe. Eventually, the German fighter units would nearly run out of effectively prepared replacement pilots, but thanks to the system established stateside, the flow of well-trained airmen never slowed to the Eighth Air Force.

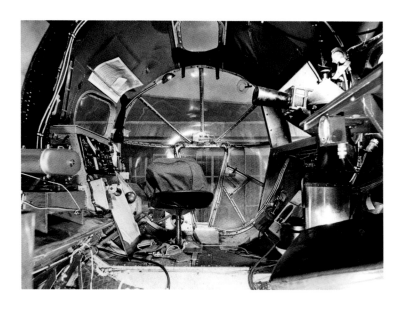

The B-17E incorporated numerous changes from the earlier variants that saw service in the Pacific and with the British. Among the most important changes was the addition of power turrets, each equipped with twin .50-caliber machine guns.

The bombardier's compartment in the nose of a B-17. Thanks to the Norden bombsight's linkage to the flight controls, the bombardier actually flew the aircraft from the initial point all the way to the release point with the assistance of an autopilot system.

THE AVRO LANCASTER

BORN FROM FAILURE, forged from experience, bought and paid for with the blood of British airmen, the Avro Lancaster emerged as one of the best heavy bombers of World War II.

When the Avro Manchester turned out to be such a disappointment, the company's engineers and designers went back to work, searching for a way to make the aircraft more effective and reliable. The Lancaster resulted from that return to the drawing board. With four engines turning four instead of two props, a longer wingspan, and other modifications, the Lancaster carried a crew of seven and a payload that could exceed twenty-two thousand pounds in certain instances. The RAF at last possessed a companion aircraft to the Halifax that could carry out the massive area bombing missions Sir Charles Portal and Bomber Harris envisioned.

The "Lanc," as the RAF's crews called it, came into service gradually through 1942. By the following year, it formed the Bomber Command's backbone. Eventually, over seven thousand were built at a cost of about fifty thousand pounds each. For Great Britain, the Lancaster program marked a prodigious expenditure of treasure and effort. Once in service, the aircraft exceeded all expectations. Over the course of the final three years of the war, Lancasters flew over 158,000 sorties over Europe and dropped 608,612 tons of bombs.

The quad .303 machine guns in the Lancaster's tail turret.

Loading a four-ton "blockbuster" bomb aboard a Lancaster. The Lanc gave the RAF a long-range aircraft capable of carrying fourteen thousand pounds of ordnance. Modified versions could carry the 22,000-pound "Grand Slam" bomb.

A formation of B-17s takes shape over England well above a near total layer of clouds. Often, weather was the strategic bombing campaign's worst enemy.

Paul Tibbets led the 97th Bomb Group's formation during the famed August 17, 1942, mission to the Rouen railroad facilities. Later, as the commander of the 509th Composite Group, he flew the *Enola Gay* to Hiroshima and dropped the world's first atomic bomb.

The Eighth Air Force's bomber crews in 1942 and early 1943 disliked bombing the German U-boat pens built in the French coastal port cities. They faced intense opposition during such attacks, and the pens were protected with reinforced concrete twenty-something-feet thick or more. The USAAF had no bomb that could penetrate such a hardened target.

"thousand plane raid." When he first floated the idea, Bomber Command possessed only about four hundred operational aircraft, the majority of which were still Wellingtons distributed among sixteen squadrons. Harris had six squadrons of Halifaxes, six more of the new and very capable Lancaster, plus two each flying Manchesters and Hampdens. To come up with the remaining aircraft for the raid, Harris had to draw on the RAF's operational training units. Instructors and student pilots would fly side-by-side on the night of this mission.

Shortly before the raid began, Harris sent a message to all his group commanders and outlined what he hoped the night's bombing would achieve.

> At best the result may bring the war to a more or less abrupt conclusion owing to the enemy's unwillingness to accept the worst that must befall him increasingly as our bomber force and that of the United States of America build up. At worst it must have the most dire moral and material effect on the enemy's war effort as a whole and force him to withdraw vast forces from his exterior aggressions for his own protection.

On the night of May 30–31, Harris gave the go-order. From fifty-three bases all over England, 1,046 bombers lifted into the darkness, bound for the Ruhr Valley industrial

General Ira Eaker at his desk. After Spaatz went to North Africa, Eaker took over command of the Eighth Air Force. He lasted about a year before he was transferred to the Med.

Operation Torch, the Allied invasion of North Africa, drew away from England and Western Europe almost all the air, naval, and ground units available to the Allies in the fall of 1942. It virtually crippled the nascent American strategic bombing campaign by absorbing almost a thousand aircraft from the Eighth Air Force and ensured the invasion of France would be delayed a year.

When the thousand-plane raid was launched against Cologne in May 1942, Bomber Command fielded thirty-seven squadrons. The Wellington equipped sixteen of them and still formed the backbone of the RAF's offensive capabilities.

After the failure of the Avro Manchester, the Lancaster emerged as the future for Bomber Command. By the time of the Cologne thousand-plane raid, Bomber Command possessed six Lancaster squadrons. After years of mediocre twin-engine and four-engine designs that proved terribly vulnerable over Germany, the RAF crews finally received an outstanding bomber with tremendous potential.

Cologne. The citizens of the city suffered terribly under the aerial punishment delivered upon their homes and factories.

city of Cologne. For hours, bombs rained down on the civilian populace. Tens of thousands took refuge in basements and cellars, bomb shelters, and other underground locations. The initial wave of attackers dropped incendiary bombs on the oldest part of the city. The flames served as a beacon for the rest of the bombers that night, and they rumbled over the city to release their loads as smoke boiled 15,000 feet into the air. The scene was soon lit with a hellish crimson glow, swathed in the acrid smoke of a city suffering immolation. The last wave of bombers could see the flames raging from over a hundred miles away.

Cologne burned and smoldered for days, making reconnaissance efforts almost useless. Finally, a week after the bombing, the first clear images of the city returned to England aboard fast-moving photo recon aircraft. The results staggered even Harris. Over six hundred acres of Cologne's downtown districts had been burnt and flattened. This represented almost thirteen thousand buildings reduced to heaps of twisted rubble. Forty-five thousand residents of the city now found themselves homeless. Another five thousand suffered death or serious injury.

Harris's optimistic view that such an attack would force an early end to the war was not realized. It didn't matter. The future had been glimpsed by both sides, and now the British devoted ever-increasing resources toward Bomber Command while the Germans raced to bolster their night fighter force.

In August, the British established their first pathfinder squadrons. These units consisted of dedicated and well-trained crews who would lead the way each night and illuminate the target area with incendiaries. Using new electronic systems, including radar, navigation became a considerably easier prospect at night. A mission to Duesseldorf in mid-September carried out by about five hundred bombers inflicted substantial damage on the city. The RAF had hit it earlier in the summer as well, yet industrial output grew 1.8 percent over the first half of the year despite all the damage and dislocation done to the city's infrastructure and factories.

In the fall, the Lancaster began to arrive in greater numbers until by October Bomber Command possessed nine squadrons totaling about a 175 planes. This was the aircraft of the future for the British strategic bombing effort. In the months to come, it would play the most vital role in nocturnal air war over Europe.

The growing attacks excited the RAF's high command and energized Churchill. That fall, the Prime Minister told President Roosevelt, "We know our night bomber offensive is having a devastating effect." The contagious optimism led Portal to conclude that the air offensive could end the war by 1944 without having to land a massive army in northwest Europe. He envisioned a campaign in 1943 and 1944 that could drop 1.25 million tons of bombs on German cities. The estimated result of such high-explosive and incendiary carnage? Portal and the Air Staff estimated it would kill nine hundred thousand German civilians, leave twenty-five million homeless and severely wound another million. The physical destruction was estimated at six million houses and near total disruption of public power and water systems, industrial capacity, and transportation routes.

The Lancaster first joined Bomber Command with 44 Squadron (pictured here) in late 1941. The unit flew its first operational sorties in the spring of 1942, just before the thousand-plane raid. Over the next three years, German defenses claimed almost 150 of 44 Squadron's Lancasters. Twenty-two more crashed in accidents. This gave the unit an attrition rate of almost 700 percent during the climactic battles of the strategic air war.

The North African campaign drained off most of the Eighth Air Force's strength in the fall of 1942. Almost thirty thousand air and ground crews were transferred to the primitive and hostile desert to join Doolittle's Twelfth Air Force.

Portal wanted to kill, wound, or dislocate 75 percent of all German citizens living in cities with populations larger than fifty thousand people. It was an extraordinary and apocalyptic vision of total war on a civilian populace. And, it was the incarnation of Douhet's central theme from *Command of the Air*.

The 1943 campaign would soon begin, and with it would come the first major contributions by the USAAF and its new fleet of heavy bombers. Exactly how that effort would be carried out in cooperation with the RAF dominated top-level discussions for the remainder of 1942, and during the Churchill-Roosevelt meeting at Casablanca in January 1943.

The RAF wanted the Americans to join the night bombing effort. Convert the Eighth Air Force to nocturnal operations and the Allies could have a force of thousands hitting Germany by moonlight before the end of 1943. The USAAF recoiled at the idea. The entire structure of its strategic force had been predicated on daylight precision bombing. All the Stateside training was geared toward this effort. Switching to night operations would require a wholesale reconstruction of the strategic bomber force. Hap Arnold, commander of the

Above: Churchill and his senior military leaders had nearly convinced FDR to switch the Eighth Air Force to night terror bombing. General Arnold tasked Ira Eaker with saving the daylight campaign. Eaker produced one of the most stunning one-page summaries of the war for Churchill, who was spellbound by its final, memorable words.

Left: FDR and his senior military leadership at Casablanca. The meeting between the Americans and British there shaped the future of the strategic air war for the next two years.

VIII FIGHTER COMMAND

"The primary role of VIII Fighter Command is to bring the bombers back alive."

GENERAL FRANK HUNTER HUNG THAT SIGN in his office when he took over VIII Fighter Command in 1942. A World War I fighter pilot, Hunter believed close escort and lots of fighter sweeps would achieve the goal he set for his pilots.

Fighter sweeps—which formed two-thirds of the missions flown by VIII Fighter Command during 1942 and part of 1943—turned out to be archaic and useless. The Germans simply would not come up and play, preferring instead to hoard their interceptor force for use against bombers.

During escort missions, Hunter repeated the errors the Germans made during the latter stages of the Battle of Britain. Chained to the bomber streams, the American fighter pilots could not even pursue Luftwaffe aircraft below 18,000 feet. With their aggressiveness negated by their tactics, the Yanks did not rack up an impressive kill ratio. The 56th Fighter Group, for example, arrived in January 1943 but did not score its first confirmed kill until June, losing a number of pilots along the way to marauding 109s and 190s.

Beyond tactical restrictions, VIII Fighter Command suffered from numerous other shortcomings. Lack of external fuel tanks crippled the fighters and restricted their radius of action to only a few hundred miles. This prevented any escort missions into Germany itself, where the majority of German interceptors waited for the bombers. As the campaign took shape, the Luftwaffe pilots simply waited until the American P-47s and P-38s turned for home before wading into the bomber stream. Yet external tanks did not gain favor until

An engine change for an Eighth Air Force Spitfire.

P-38s of the 338th Fighter Squadron, 55th Fighter Group, on their airfield in East Anglia. The 55th Fighter Group flew Lightning until converting to P-51 Mustangs in late 1944.

A 31st Fighter Group Spitfire in England. The 31st flew missions over Dieppe in August 1942 before getting sent to North Africa to aid in the effort to knock the Axis out of Tunisia. They were part of the massive drain of aircraft that left the Mighty Eighth little more than a skeletal force in late 1942.

mid-1943. To the USAAF's materials command, hanging gas tanks under a fighter was an anathema that would ruin the aircraft's maneuverability in combat.

It would take time to sort out the fuel tank issue and the tactics. In the meantime, the B-17 and B-24 crews paid the price. The 1943 campaign would prove once and for all that if the bombers were to survive deep penetration raids into Germany, the Mighty Eighth had to have fighters that could go the distance with them. Wartime experience proved Billy Mitchell right: fighter and bomber had to work together just like combined operations in ground warfare. The cost to learn that lesson envisioned two decades before by America's most famous airpower theorist would be dreadfully high.

The Republic P-47 Thunderbolt rounded out the types of fighters available to the Eighth Air Force in 1942 and early 1943. Rugged and huge, its pilots dubbed it "the Jug" for its resembled to a milk jug on wheels when sitting on the ground. Early variants sucked gas like a Hummer and could not escort the Eighth's bombers much beyond two hundred miles. That would change in the years to come, but in 1942 its lack of radius severely limited its usefulness in the strategic air war.

Eaker's synopsis concluded, "If the RAF continues bombing at night and we bomb by day, we shall bomb them round the clock and the devil shall do the rest." Churchill conferred with FDR, and the twenty-four-hour bombing campaign became the strategy to emerge from Casablanca.

USAAF, could not let that happen. Yet, Churchill had already nearly sold Roosevelt on the idea of doing this.

During the Casablanca conference in January, he cabled Eaker and told him it was up to him to save the daylight bombing campaign. Eaker had majored in journalism in college. He sat down and drafted a tight, one-page summary for Churchill that outlined all the reasons why converting the Eighth Air Force to night operations would be folly. The final sentence captured the Prime Minister's imagination.

Eaker (left) shakes hands with General Kenney, the officer who translated Douhet's classic *Command of the Air* for an American audience. Eaker's genius with words (he had been a journalism major in college) ensured the survival of the daylight bombing campaign. In a twist of irony, he himself would not survive the year as the commander of the Eighth Air Force.

"If the RAF continues bombing at night and we bomb by day, we shall bomb them round the clock and the devil shall do the rest."

Both leaders loved the idea of "round the clock bombing." The British would batter the Germans at night while from dawn to sunset the Americans would rule the skies. Twenty-four seven, Germany would receive no respite from the aerial bombardment.

After Casablanca, Eaker and one of his subordinates, General Hansell, sat down with two RAF counterparts and drafted a detailed plan for the 1943 air campaign. Called the Combined Bomber Offensive, the document set seventeen key target types to be attacked and destroyed during the year. The top three included: 1) the German aircraft industry, 2) ball bearings factories, and 3) Germany's oil refining infrastructure. Harris and Bomber Command would still make destruction of German morale its key objective for the year.

For both sides, 1943 would be a pivotal period in the strategic air war. Of course, as with most wartime ventures, nothing went as planned.

General Hap Arnold shakes hands with an aviator in the MTO while General Spaatz looks on. Arnold kept a very close eye on the strategic air war in Europe, considering it the USAAF's main effort in World War II.

Bombing up an Eighth Air Force Fort prior to a mission in 1943.

6

POINTBLANK BEGINS

★ ★ ★ ★ ★

I saw a Fort knocked out of the group
On fire and in despair
With Nazi fighters surrounding her
As it flew alone back there.

The Messerschmitts came barreling through
Throwin' a hail of lead
At the crippled Fort that wouldn't quit
Though two of its engines were dead.
But a couple of props kept straining away
And her guns were blazing too
As she stayed in the air
In that hell back there
And fought as Fortresses do.
—Anonymous Eighth Air Force crewman, penned while in captivity
in Stalag Luft #1. *Quoted in* Staying Alive *by Maj. Carl Fyler*

An Eighth Air Force raid en route to Bremen. Bremen was one of the nail-biter missions for the crews. Thoroughly defended by flak and fighters, the city was home to aircraft factories and U-boat construction facilities. Losses on such raids were heavy throughout 1943.

BREMEN WAS ONE OF THOSE TARGETS that made the American bomber crews groan. The factories in Bremen gave birth to many of the Focke-Wulf 190s that intercepted their formations to kill and wound their friends. The Germans ringed Bremen with heavy anti-aircraft guns and a concentration of fighters that made every raid on the city a harrowing ordeal for the Mighty Eighth.

On April 17, 1943, Eaker sent his men against Bremen. Four bomb groups, led by the 91st's twenty-eight B-17s, formed up

The U-boat yard at Bremen was a priority Eighth Air Force target, one that was repeatedly bombed through 1943 and 1944.

over East Anglia and headed for their target. The force totaled 107 bombers. Back at the 91st Group's base at Bassingbourn, the commanding officer had arranged to host a huge party that evening that included 150 civilian guests and 200 men from the group.

Near the target area, the Germans coordinated a masterful interception. The Messerschmitts and Focke-Wulfs concentrated on the 91st and made determined head-on attacks against its squadrons. Six of its Forts went down in flames—five from one squadron. Most of the 91st's remaining planes suffered damage. Altogether, fifteen Forts fell to the German fighters. Another thirty-nine returned home scarred by flak shrapnel, cannon shells, and machine gun hits. Over half the attacking force went down or took damage. It was a desperate and sobering moment for the Eighth Air Force.

At Bassingbourn, the partiers awaited the 91st Group's return. They straggled in, dead aboard their battered Forts. In horror, many of the guests realized that the men who had invited them had died that afternoon over Germany. As the survivors climbed out of their aircraft, most wanted nothing to do with the festivities.

The party went on. The men showed up, nerves shot from the ordeal they'd just experienced. The mood only grew worse as the alcohol flowed and the evening wore on. The survivors drank away their pain and some got so out of control that the group's historian recorded the event for posterity, noting that "several of the combat crew members indulged too freely."

Bremen set the tone for a year of catastrophes and casualties. On June 13, the heavies struck at Kiel and Bremen simultaneously with 182 aircraft. The Germans shot 22 of them out of the sky and damaged another 23. Such losses simply could not be sustained. The crews began to suffer the effects of prolonged exposure to the stress of combat. They had trouble sleeping. They self-medicated with alcohol. Some broke down completely and had to be grounded. A few committed suicide rather than face the crucible of flak and fighters again.

Three days before that dreadful mission, the U.S. chiefs of staff issued the Eighth its marching orders in what became known as Directive Pointblank. Taken straight from the Combined Bomber Operations document Eaker, Hansell, and the British produced, Pointblank called for the destruction of the German aircraft industry and the simultaneous seizure of air superiority over Western Europe. It was a tall order. That summer, the Germans had put their aircraft factories in high gear. That spring, the workers in those plants constructed over a thousand fighters a month. The total Luftwaffe fighter force rose from about 1,600 planes in February to over 2,000 by the start of the summer. Of those, about 800 defended the Reich and its Western approaches from the Eighth Air Force.

Bad weather hampered the execution of Pointblank for over a month. Finally, toward the end of July, the clouds vanished and blue skies greeted the bomber crews each dawn. Eaker

A 95th Bomb Group B-17 struggles through a sky full of 88mm flak bursts over Bremen.

seized the moment. In what became known as "Blitz Week" the Eighth flew maximum effort missions for six consecutive days starting on July 25. Hamburg served as the first target of the new offensive. The target had been chosen jointly with Bomber Command in what became one of the first incidents of round-the-clock bombing on a German city. The night before, Bomber Command hit the city with incendiaries and 4,000-pound blockbuster bombs. The next morning, The Eighth attacked Hamburg's shipyards. Frantic Luftwaffe interceptors pressed their attacks to point-blank range over the burning city and blew fifteen American bombers out of the air. Sixty-seven more suffered serious damage out of the hundred that made it to the Initial Point (IP), the start of the bomb run.

The following night, the British bombed Hamburg again, but thunderstorms disrupted the mission. They tried again on the night of the twenty-seventh, sending 739 bombers through the darkened skies to Hamburg. With the air dry and warm, the incendiary attack created a tornado of fire that stretched a thousand feet into the air. The flames, whipped and propelled by winds of over 150 miles an hour, consumed eight square miles of downtown Hamburg. The firestorm melted asphalt, asphyxiated hundreds of civilians trapped in underground shelters, and burned everything in its path. Witnesses reported seeing the hurricane-like winds sweep people right off the streets and throw them into the roiling flames. Bomber Command hit the city two more times before August 3. When the operation ended,

Unlike the RAF's night campaign, there was no hiding in the daylight skies over Western Europe. Early on, the Eighth Air Force crews discovered their aircraft left contrails that could be seen for dozens of miles. Luftwaffe fighters had little trouble locating them once their ground controllers vectored them into the bomber stream's general vicinity.

A 91st Bomb Group Fort swings low over an airfield in East Anglia after a mission over Europe in September 1943.

Eighth Air Force Bases and Air Divisions

The Wash

Spalding

King's Lynn

Attlebridge (120)　Horsham St. Faith (120)
(118) Wendling　(125) Rackheath

North Pickenham (143)　(115) Shipdham　Norwich
2nd AD

Wisbech

Stamford　Great Yarmouth

Downham Market　Bodney (141)　(376) Watton
(142) Deopham Green　(114) Hethel　(146) Seething

Peterborough　*Nene*　March

Deenethorpe (367) King's Cliff　Attleborough
Snetterton Heath (138)　Old Buckenham (144)　(104)　Lowestof
(128)　Whittlesey　East Wretham (133)　Tibbenham (144) Hardwick　(125) Bungay (Flixton)

Corby　Polebrook (110)　Chatteris　Thetford　Thorpe Abbotts (139)　(366) Metfield
(130) Glatton　Ely　Honington (375) Knettishall (136)　Diss　(365) Halesworth

Grafton Underwood (106)　Molesworth (107)　Alconbury (102)　Middleham　Eye (134)
　　　Huntingdon　　　Bury St. Edmunds　(119) Horham

Chelveston (105)　(117) Kimbolton　Newmarket　Great Ashfield (155)　(156) Mendlesham　(153)　(373) Leiston

Podlington (109)　*Cam*　(374) Bottisham　(468) Rougham
(111) Thurleigh　Cambridge　Rattlesden (126)　Framlingham
Bedford　(377) Wattisham　(152) Debach

Fowlmer　Lavenham (137)　**3rd AD**　(369) Martlesham Heath
Basingbourn (378) (357) Duxford　Ridgewell
(121)　(174) Sudbury　Ipswich
Steeple Morden (122)　(165) Little Walden　(167)　(157) Raydon
Milton Keynes　Saffron Walden　　Felixstowe

Letchworth　(356) Debden　Wormingford (159)　Harwich
(131)　Earl's Colne (358)　(150) Boxted
Hitchin　Nuthampstead
Stevenage　Bishop's Stortford　Great Saling (475)　Colchester
Luton (113) Cheddington　　(Adnrew's Field)　Braintree
Aylesbury　Hartford　Witham　Clacton on Sea

Bovingdon (112)　St. Albans　Chelmsford

Watford

Beaconsfield　Rayleigh
Basildon　Southend

LONDON

Stains　Grays
Gravesend　Margate
Rochester　Chatham　Ramsgate
Epsom　Faversham
Woking　Maidstone　Canterbury
Sevenoaks

Dorking　Reigate

Thames

N O R T H

S E A

(167) Airfield and station number

0　10　20　30 miles

As a stopgap, the Eighth Air Force experimented with YB-40 escort bombers to protect its Flying Fort formations. The YB-40 was an up-armored B-17 loaded with extra ammunition and .50-caliber machine guns. In combat, they proved to be nearly useless and were so laden that they could not stay in formation with the more lightly loaded B-17s after they had emptied their bomb bays. These YB-40s belonged to the 91st Bomb Group.

over fifty thousand German civilians lay dead in the smoldering ruins of their city. A million more emerged from their shelters to find their homes destroyed.

While Bomber Command devastated Hamburg, the Eighth's "Blitz Week" continued. On the twenty-sixth, the Forts and Liberators hit Hanover and Hamburg again; 227 American airmen died, went missing, or suffered wounds during those twin raids.

In the first two days of Blitz Week, the Eighth lost 317 men. Eaker did not ease up on the operational tempo. On the twenty-eighth, the bombers struck the Fieseler aircraft factory in Kassel and another aviation plant at Oschersleben. Over three hundred bombers left East Anglia. Twenty-two went down over Europe and over a hundred more returned to England with battle damage. Another 231 airmen became casualties.

During the day's missions, the Germans unleashed a new surprise on the American bomber crews. This time, deep over the Third Reich, the B-17 formations encountered a formation of Messerschmitt Bf-110 fighters equipped with rocket projectors under their

The 351st Bomb Group en route to a target inside Germany during the 1943 campaign.

A target photo showing the 303rd Bomb Group's tight pattern of 500-pound bombs walking across the hangar and barracks facilities at a Luftwaffe airfield outside of Orleans, France.

Above: Summer at Molesworth Airfield in East Anglia, home of the 303rd Bomb Group. Many of the Eighth Air Force stations were carved straight out of the farmland in the area. The local farmers would continue to work the land surrounding the facilities, leading to fall harvests as the Americans continued the air war against Germany.

Left: Ground crews frequently decorated bombs bound for the Third Reich with typical irreverent American humor.

A formation of Eighth Air Force Forts in 1943. The nose armament ended up being the weak point of the B-17E and F models. When the Luftwaffe discovered this, the best Jagdgeschwaders executed head-on passes through the bomber boxes.

wings. Called the Gr.21, the new weapon was an adaptation of a Wehrmacht infantry mortar. The 110s lurked behind the 385th Bomb Group, their pilots careful to stay out of machine gun range as they launched their rockets. The projectiles shot out of their tubes, soared over the 385th's aircraft, then fell right into the middle of their formation and exploded. The attack scored a direct hit on a B-17, which spun into two others and sent them plummeting earthward in flames. In a heartbeat, the 385th lost thirty men.

July 29, 1943, saw Eaker send his units against Kiel and the Heinkel factory at Warnemünde. The effort that day claimed another hundred American airmen. And still Eaker would not ease up on the pace. Over a hundred more men went down the next day over Kassel.

So much bloodshed, so many aircraft lost—to what gain? Post strike reconnaissance showed spotty accuracy at best. In order to get their bombs to their intended destination, the Forts and Liberator crews had to fly straight and level from the IP until they reached the target. This usually required flying without any evasive maneuvers at all for at least fifteen miles at a time when the crews usually faced the heaviest concentrations of anti-aircraft fire.

continued on page 121

A B-17 navigator at work in his cramped compartment.

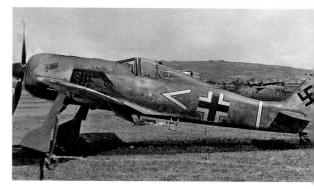

The dreaded "Butcher Bird"—the Focke-Wulf Fw-190A, the Luftwaffe's most deadly daylight interceptor in 1943. Standard armament included four 20mm cannons and a pair of machine guns firing over the nose. Later, the Germans manufactured underwing 20mm packages that could double the Focke-Wulf's cannon firepower. In such a configuration, the Focke-Wulf became a deadly bomber destroyer. But those extra cannons came at the expense of maneuverability, however, and if caught by American escort fighters they were easy prey.

Based mainly inside the Third Reich itself, out of range of VIII Fighter Command's aircraft, the Luftwaffe's heavy fighters, like this Messerschmitt Me-410, used rockets to disrupt B-17 formations before closing in and picking off stragglers with cannon fire. They were the most effective casualty-producing interceptor in the skies during 1943 and helped tip the scales in favor of the Luftwaffe later that fall.

Hit by flak over Trondheim, Norway, an Eighth Air Force B-17 falls out of formation over the North Sea. The combat box provided safety and mutual defense. When a damaged B-17 could not keep up with its squadron mates, chances were good marauding Luftwaffe fighters would pounce on them and finish the crippled aircraft off.

A 385th Bomb Group crew drags a damaged Fort home as "meat wagons"—ambulances—await its landing.

"This is It," a 381st Bomb Group Flying Fort on a bomb run over Mainz, Germany. The final approach to a target area was always the most vulnerable moments for the Eighth Air Force crews. To ensure maximum accuracy, the Forts and Liberators had to fly straight and level for at least fifteen miles while the lead bombardiers located and tracked the target. The Germans recognized this as the killing moments and ringed vital installations with heavy flak batteries. If the flak didn't actually knock aircraft down, it frequently disrupted formations enough to degrade accuracy.

A B-17 combat box over France in 1943. The German fighter pilots learned to judge which groups were better than others by how tight the pilots stayed in these formations. Less experienced crews tended to fly in looser boxes, which the Luftwaffe would exploit with sudden, slashing attacks at their weakest points.

A captured Fw-190A under flight testing back in the United States. The USAAF thoroughly evaluated the Focke-Wulf to learn its weaknesses and strengths so that tactics could be developed to defeat this very effective German fighter.

Shot up and on fire with three engines out, this B-17's crew managed to limp back to East Anglia and crash-land in rolling farmland, where Eighth Air Force ground personnel caught up to it and began effecting repairs. Such incidents were all too common through the 1943 campaign.

The tail gunner's positing in a 91st Bomb Group B-17 at Bassingbourn in 1943. The twin .50-caliber machine guns proved so effective when groups massed into their protective combat boxes that the Luftwaffe interceptors virtually gave up stern attacks.

The Fort's weak nose armament—a single hand-held .50 used by the bombardier—was soon discovered and exploited by the Luftwaffe's fighter pilots. To counter their head-on attack tactics, the Eighth Air Force groups began field-modifying their aircraft. In this case, the ground crews of the 91st Bomb Group installed a twin .50 mount in the nose of a B-17 at Bassingbourn in February 1943.

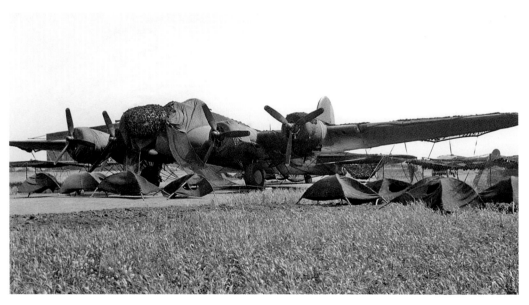

Above: Eaker and Gen. Jacob Devers pose beneath the nose of the most famous Eighth Air Force B-17—the *Memphis Belle*. The crew of the *Memphis Belle* became the first to complete their twenty-five-mission tour in England.

Left: In May 1943, Luftwaffe reconnaissance aircraft and occasional bombing raids on England remained a threat. Here, the 92nd Bomb Group has covered one of its Forts with camouflage netting. Pup tents for the ground crews surround the aircraft.

Morning at Ridgewell, home of the 381st Bomb Group, in August 1943.

Most groups simply abandoned that SOP (standard operating procedure). Even after the IP had been reached, they would change altitude every few seconds to throw off the radar-operated guns below them. The Norden sights could not handle such maneuvers and still make its calculations with any accuracy. Fewer Forts went down, but the targets remained intact, which required return visits to them and more exposure to Luftwaffe interceptors. It was a zero-sum game with the crews caught in a hellish cycle.

In 1942, the average Eighth Air Force bomber crew could expect to survive about fourteen or fifteen missions. Twenty-five completed a tour. Not many did. They faced long odds that year. In the summer of 1943, the odds grew even worse. The average crew survived fewer than ten missions.

As Blitz Week came to its bloody end, there was no doubt who was winning the air war over Germany: the Luftwaffe still controlled the daylight skies.

Caught from behind by an Eighth Air Force fighter, a Focke-Wulf Fw-190 pilot breaks right in a desperate effort to get out of his pursuer's line of fire. He was a split second too late, and the American's bullets can be seen scoring hits along the right wing root.

A pair of 305th Bomb Group B-17s prepare for takeoff at Chelveston in June 1943. The Eighth Air Force had grown strong enough that summer to challenge the Luftwaffe over the Third Reich for the first time. Without a long-range escort fighter to protect them, the Eighth's bombers took a serious beating.

Members of the 376th Bomb Group pose before one of their B-24Ds. Known as the Liberandos, the 376th was one of only two heavy bombardment groups in Brereton's Ninth Air Force.

7

THE GET RICH QUICK SCHEME

THE USAAF'S STRATEGIC BOMBING DEVOTEES understood that to destroy the Third Reich's military industrial complex would require a long campaign whose success would not be quantifiable until long after the war ended. At least, intellectually they understood this. Viscerally, the targeting experts and planners continually sought to deliver a single body blow to the Reich's war making capabilities that could materially affect the strategic situation in the moment, not six months down the road. It would take three painful lessons and well over a thousand fine young men to finally drive this fantasy from the ranks of the USAAF's senior brass. By the late fall of 1943, it was obvious to everyone that there was no super-target that could drive Hitler's air force and armies to their knees.

At first glance, it is easy to see why such a visceral desire lingered. Colonel Richard Hughes, the Eighth Air Force targeting expert, had studied the Reich's economy with his staff to develop a prioritized list of industrial facilities to be bombed. Several stuck out, including the massive ball-bearings complex at Schweinfurt, the aircraft factories at Regensburg and Wiener-Neustadt, and the oil refineries of Ploesti. In each case, these plants formed a significant percentage of the production in their respective fields. If they could be knocked out, the effect could be immediate.

Ploesti looked to be among the most promising. The various refining facilities there provided the Third Reich with 35 percent of its refined oil. Such a huge concentration of production capacity had to become a key target for any serious strategic bombing campaign, but by the summer of 1943, the Allies had attacked Ploesti only three times. The Russians had launched two nuisance raids, and the Americans had attacked it with an inconsequential number of B-24 Liberators based in North Africa.

The Eighth Air Force units were accustomed to the weather and conditions in England. The Libyan desert's primitive conditions and minimal logistical support seriously complicated preparations for Tidal Wave. Here, members of the 93rd Bomb Group prepare a bomb prior to a mission in the cold morning air in England before deploying to Libya. Just the aircraft made the trip to the North African desert, forcing the Eighth Air Force groups to rely on the Ninth Air Force ground crews to service, arm, and fuel their B-24s.

The 343rd Bomb Squadron of Col. John Kane's 98th Group painted their aircraft in a *Snow White and the Seven Dwarfs* theme. The 98th was fortunate to have a talented artist named Amos Nicholson serving with the ground crew. His inspired nose art has captured the eye of generations of collectors and historians. This particular B-24, *Dopey*, miraculously survived the war, only to be condemned and scrapped in the late fall of 1945.

Prince Charming, another 343rd Bomb Squadron B-24D, was flown by Lt. Thomas Bennett during Operation Tidal Wave. It was one of the eight aircraft that aborted due to mechanical failure prior to reaching the Balkan coast.

There were a number of problems with attacking Ploesti. At the top of that list was its location deep in Romania. Out of range from England, using the Eighth Air Force was not an option. That left Gen. Louis Brereton's Ninth Air Force, stationed in Libya. Even so, such an attack would stretch Brereton's already over tasked B-24 Liberator units. Getting there and back would require a 2,700 mile flight, much of it through an air defense network bristling with anti-aircraft artillery, supported by an outstanding radar and observation network and backed up by over three hundred Axis interceptors. Due to the ranges involved, any attacking

Snow White and the Seven Dwarfs was piloted by Lt. James A. Gunn III. After following Colonel Kane into Ploesti and dropping their bombs on target, Gunn's crew ran into a flight of Bf-109 interceptors from JG-27. The 109s knocked Gunn's aircraft down west of Kefalonia Island, Greece, killing eight of the nine men on board. One member of the crew survived to be captured by the Germans.

Allied force would have to go in without escort fighters riding shotgun during the bomb runs. In any scenario, rolling in over Ploesti at 20,000 feet at 180 miles an hour would be a near-suicidal aerial parade across the Balkans.

Brereton had precisely two bomb groups: the 376th "Liberandos" and the 98th "Pyramiders." Without massive reinforcements, bombing Ploesti would have to remain a distant pipe dream.

After the Casablanca Conference in early 1943, one of Gen. Hap Arnold's trusted inner circle, Col. Jacob Smart, happened to attend a training exercise that involved a formation of A-20 Havocs attacking vehicles. The Havoc pilots came in low on the deck and nailed their targets with such deadly accuracy that it got Smart's wheels turning. If the light attack boys

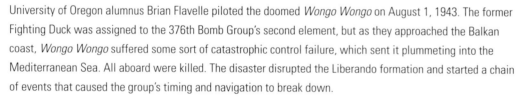

University of Oregon alumnus Brian Flavelle piloted the doomed *Wongo Wongo* on August 1, 1943. The former Fighting Duck was assigned to the 376th Bomb Group's second element, but as they approached the Balkan coast, *Wongo Wongo* suffered some sort of catastrophic control failure, which sent it plummeting into the Mediterranean Sea. All aboard were killed. The disaster disrupted the Liberando formation and started a chain of events that caused the group's timing and navigation to break down.

The primitive, harsh conditions of the Libyan desert defied the traditional image of the aviator's cushy life in World War II. Tents, desert sand, and terrible food and water were the order of the day for the men. A lack of hangars, spare parts, and logistical support facilities, like proper bomb storage magazines, played havoc with the ground crews, who had to work in the open under the blazing North African sun day after day just to keep the bombers flying.

could wreak such destruction, even if it was in a simulated environment, what could a low-flying strategic bomber do?

This was not a novel idea. In Kenney's Fifth Air Force, the B-24 and B-17 groups had been running low altitude attacks on Japanese shipping for months with good results. Could it be done against strategic targets? The question intrigued Smart.

All of thirty-three years old, Smart had replaced Lauris Norstad on Arnold's Advisory Council in mid-1942 after Norstad was sent overseas to serve as Jimmy Doolittle's chief of staff in the Twelfth Air Force. The Advisory Council functioned as Arnold's brain trust, conceiving long-range plans while functioning as the communications conduit between the meeting-averse Arnold and the Air Staff. The young, capable officers on the Advisory Council had Arnold's ear, and had the potential to greatly influence how the USAAF was employed across the globe.

Nowhere is that more evident than in the genesis of Operation Tidal Wave. After Smart's epiphany on the training range marveling at the deftly handled A-20s as they roared low overhead, he proposed that Brereton's bombers hit Ploesti in the same way. There were reasons to like the plan. First, by staying low the Liberators could stay undetected by German radar. That could give the strike force an edge of surprise that would minimize casualties. Going in on the deck would also maximize bombing accuracy and the damage the B-24s

Ploesti was the most heavily defended target in Southern Europe in the summer of 1943. Some 300 anti-artillery guns and 320 interceptors guarded the oil refineries. The Germans used flak trains to quickly shift their anti-aircraft assets from one threatened target to another around the Ploesti complex. Here, a flak train mounts heavy 128mm guns. During Tidal Wave, the B-24 gunners fought a desperate, point blank gunfight with these trains as they sped along at low altitude.

Another example of a German 128mm anti-aircraft gun, this one emplaced in a fixed position. Capable of reaching any altitude Allied bombers could attain, the 128 provided the perfect heavy flak support to the more numerous and famous 88s.

could inflict on the target area. In that sort of scenario, a smaller force could do more damage down low than a massive one from 20,000 feet.

Smart took his idea to Arnold, who loved it. Soon, the concept had the approval of the Air Staff and the Joint Chiefs of Staff. It was so wild and innovative that FDR was smitten by it as well. He loved the unorthodox, and Smart's idea flaunted all doctrine and broke every prewar rule.

Clearly, two groups of B-24s that had been operating out of the Western Desert for months would not be enough. They weren't at full strength, and fifty bombers would not be sufficient to get the job done anyway. For this one raid, the Eighth Air Force would have to lend Brereton three bomb groups. Not surprisingly, Ira Eaker howled in protest at the dispersion of his scant resources. He'd already lost several B-17 groups to Doolittle's Twelfth Air Force. Now he was asked to siphon away even more men and planes, even if it were temporary.

There were other opponents in theater as well. Colonel Hughes didn't like the plan. Neither did Gen. Gordon Saville, Spaatz's chief of staff at Mediterranean Air Command.

A 44th Bomb Group B-24D. The 44th had trained in Washington at McChord Field before moving to Oklahoma for its final pre-deployment training. Assigned to the Eighth Air Force, the 44th became one of the early B-24 groups to operate in England. To bolster General Brereton's B-24 strength for the Ploesti Raid, the 44th, 389th, and 93rd Bomb Groups were redeployed to the Libyan desert in the early summer of 1943. After Operation Tidal Wave, the 44th returned to England and operated for the duration of the war with the Mighty Eighth. This particular B-24 was shot down in May 1943 while serving with the 68th Bomb Squadron.

Louis Brereton loved the idea and completely embraced it. His Ninth Air Force would be in the limelight, and the potential of delivering a catastrophic blow to the Third Reich captivated his imagination. His enthusiasm drove the ultimate execution of what became known as Operation Tidal Wave.

Starting on July 19, 1943, the B-24 groups began rehearsals for the attack. Navigating at low altitude took a lot of skill and practice, so the squadrons kicked off a crash course in it. Out in the Libyan desert, Brereton's command constructed a mock up of the Ploesti area complete with white-washed outlines of buildings and landmarks and gasoline drums serving as stand-ins for the oil storage tanks at each of the seven refineries on the target list. Every day, the groups practiced formation flying on the deck while finding the target area out in the desert. As they did, more resistance to the plan developed.

General Uzal Ent, head of 9th Bomber Command, tried to get Tidal Wave altered so his men could go in at high altitude as they had trained all their USAAF careers to do. A few days of rehearsals would not prepare his men for the trial ahead. He was ignored. Worried, he elected to join his men on the mission, and when the 376th Bomb Group lifted off their dusty Libyan airfield, Ent was riding with the group's commanding officer, Colonel Keith Compton.

More concern came from Ike and Tedder, both of whom urged Brereton to cancel the mission. If only they had made that an order.

August 1, 1943: five groups of B-24D Liberators arose in the early hours of dawn to face curtains of flak and diving interceptors. The 376th took station as the lead group. Colonel Compton's ride, *Teggie Ann*, formed the point of a spear 176 Liberators strong. Behind

Anxious ground crew await the return of the Tidal Wave strike force. When the battle-damaged B-24s limped back to Libya, the full cost of the raid slowly dawned on those left behind. There would be dreadfully large gaps around the tables in the chow tent that night.

the Liberandos came the Pyramiders of Col. John "Killer" Kane's 98th Bomb Group, and the 44th, 389th, and 93rd groups as well.

Over the Med, the first Liberators began to abort. Mechanical issues claimed eleven of the bombers, and they limped back to the desert to find their airfields. At 1130 that morning, the first disaster struck. Flying in the Liberandos' second element was *Wongo Wongo*, a B-24D flown by University of Oregon graduate Brian Flavelle. For reasons never determined, his Liberator suddenly jerked out of formation and staggered erratically through the air. The entire element broke apart as the other pilots sought to avoid a mid-air collision with *Wongo Wongo*. Flavelle and his copilot must have fought the controls, but it was no use. Their B-24 plunged straight into the Mediterranean off the coast of Corfu, killing all ten aboard. Flavelle's wingman dove down and circled the area in hopes of spotting survivors, but the effort was in vain.

Many accounts of Tidal Wave point to this moment as the one that unraveled the entire operation. Flavelle's plane supposedly carried the lead navigator for the mission, and with his death the 376th ended up off course. Recent scholarship has shown this probably was not the case. The lead navigator was with Colonel Compton and General Ent in *Teggie Ann* at the head of the strike formation. There is no doubt losing Flavelle to some sort of malfunction affected the Liberandos, but what happened next can't be blamed on his loss.

The Liberators reached the Balkan coast like an onrushing earthquake. Their passage shook the ground for miles as 656 Pratt & Whitney R-1830s blasted the pastoral scenes below with 787, 200 combined horsepower. It must have been an unforgettable sight to those on the ground who witnessed it.

Over mountains the bombers skimmed, racing against not just the Axis air defense network, but against the complex timing of the attack as well. Tidal Wave called for near-simultaneous attacks on all seven refineries around Ploesti. Since there were only five bomb groups, several of the targets would be hit with less than optimal numbers. The plan called for simultaneous runs on all seven facilities. Already, the chaos over the Med caused by

The Liberandos return home to Libya. Eight of the group's B-24s were lost that day.

A B-24 roars low over the target area, engulfed by the chaos of flames, smoke, and flak.

Preparing a 500-pound bomb in the desert was a very elemental affair. Without proper equipment, the ground crews improvised and made it work.

Flavelle's loss had compromised the timing for the 376th. Now, as the Liberandos reached what Colonel Compton thought was their IP, another critical mistake was made.

Compton turned too early. The plan called for the bombers to fly northwest of Ploesti, then swing right and descend on the target area from an unexpected direction. Instead of that happening, Colonel Compton's premature turn set the Liberandos on a direct course to Bucharest, over thirty miles south of Ploesti.

A crew from the 376th Bomb Group reaches their aircraft in the predawn hours before the go-order was given and the Ploesti strike launched. During their pre-mission briefings, the air crew were shown a specially made film about Ploesti. It started with the narrator saying, "Ploesti is a virgin target . . . " while depicting a supple half-naked young woman.

Many of the group's navigators soon detected the error. Radio silence was broken as they called out, "Mistake! Mistake!" over the command net. Compton pushed on, directly into the heaviest concentration of anti-aircraft guns in Europe. The German defenders had calculated an attack on Ploesti would have to come from the south, given the fuel considerations the Americans had to take into account. The southern corridor into Ploesti was lined with AAA.

Meanwhile, one B-24, *Brewery Wagon*, broke out of the Liberando formation and turned for Ploesti. Alone, it waded into the target area leaping over fences, telephone poles, and buildings like a hurdler at a track meet. Flak filled the skies around the B-24 until an 88mm shell struck its nose and killed the plane's navigator and bombardier. Crippled, the pilot

A Liberando B-24 returns home. The Ploesti raid cost the USAAF over five hundred men.

dumped his bombs to stay aloft. Moments later, a Messerschmitt Bf-109 spotted them and dove for the kill. The interceptors finished what the flak gunners started. *Brewery Wagon* slammed into the ground. German and Romanian soldiers surrounded and captured them within minutes.

Just as the rest of the 376th Bomb Group reached the outskirts of Bucharest, Colonel Compton realized his mistake and ordered a sharp left turn to the north. Instead of coming in to Ploesti running northwest to southeast like the rest of the strike force, the Liberandos flew straight into the teeth of the most heavily defended sectors around Ploesti racing south to north. They crossed paths with the other B-24s in a flaming chaos over the target area.

Only the 98th Bomb Group maintained its schedule and appropriate course. Coming into the target area, Kane had already lost eight of his aircraft to mechanical aborts. Now down to a skeleton crew, he could see smoke boiling up from the refineries. Other units had already attacked. At that moment, a flight of 376th Bomb Group B-24s suddenly appeared *below* Kane's aircraft, *Hail Columbia*, streaking off target before turning for home.

The sky filled with anti-aircraft fire. Ahead, a haystack on the edge of the refineries suddenly melted away to reveal a flak gun. Kane dove below the tree line and used the two fixed-forward firing .50 calibers to "shoot my way in." Before even reaching the target, he'd fired all 2,400 rounds of ready ammunition for the guns, leaving his navigator knee deep in sizzling, spent shell casings.

To the right of Kane's flight a flak train appeared. Armed with 88mm and 128mm heavy guns, the train rolled parallel to the 98th Bomb Group's course and hammered the

Sandman, a 98th Bomb Group Liberator flown by Lt. Robert Sternfels, skims across the smoke and flames of the Astra Romana Refinery at the height of the Tidal Wave attack. Sternfels and his crew could not make it back across the Med after exiting the target area. Instead, they diverted to the RAF field on Cyprus.

formation with point blank fire. The fusillade was so accurate that two of Kane's B-24s, including his wingman, took hits that killed two men and wounded another. A third Liberator had an engine shot out. The German and American gunners traded fire in one of history's most unusual drive by shootings, and for interminable seconds the planes and train dueled to the death.

Overhead, a squadron of German Messerschmitt Bf-109s spotted Kane's group rushing forward on their final approach to their target area in five waves. Diving down into their own flak, the interceptors played havoc with the Liberators. Kane's flight leader in the fifth wave went down, victim to both flak and fighters.

At this point, Kane could have aborted the mission. The furious reception, the devastating losses already suffered by the unit through aborts and battle damage had thinned the 98th's already stretched ranks. All Kane had to do was radio the code word "crabapple" and the Pyramiders would break contact and speed for home.

He did not give that code word. Instead, throttles firewalled, his B-24 plunged into the tempest of flames, flak and smoke over the target. Colonel Kane led the way across the Phoenix Orion

THE B-24

WHEN CONSOLIDATED conceived and constructed the B-24, they chose a path of function over form. Ugly, box-like, and looking like a duck with its shoulders around its ears, the Liberator inspired none of the aesthetic pleasure that defined the B-17 Flying Fortress. Yet, it could carry a heavier bomb load than the Fort over a longer distance. In time, it outstripped the B-17 as the mainstay of America's strategic bombing force. Over sixteen thousand—double the number of B-17s—rolled off stateside production lines by war's end.

The Liberator was not without its issues. First, its narrow, long wings did not lend themselves to close formation flying at high altitudes. While the Forts remained rock solid and easy to keep tucked into a group defensive box above 20,000 feet, fully loaded Liberators tended to wallow around. This had profound consequences over Germany, as the Luftwaffe preyed on groups displaying looser formations. The more spread out the bombers were, the less able they became at mutually supporting defensive fire. Liberator groups took heavy losses at times because of this design deficiency.

The Liberator also lacked the Fort's rugged construction, a fact that did nothing to endear the B-24 to its crews. It was the ultimate utilitarian bomber of World War II, a workhorse, never beloved or revered, but one that carried the war to the heart of the Third Reich by 1944.

What passed for amenities in the Libyan desert. The men of the heavy bombardment groups suffered from an array of diseases, including dysentery, due to the Stone Age quality of their living conditions.

The 98th and 476th Bomb Groups had been heavily engaged throughout 1943 in the lead up to Tidal Wave. During July, the two groups supported Operation Husky, the invasion of Sicily, before switching into training mode for the Ploesti attack. Despite the almost catastrophic casualty rate over the Balkans, the B-24 groups returned to Nazi-dominated skies in the immediate aftermath of the raid. The pressure on the crews could not have been more intense.

refinery, one of Ploesti's seven facilities, when one of the huge storage tanks took a bomb hit and exploded. A shaft of flames erupted from the tank, blowing the saucer-shaped lid hundreds of feet into the air. Moments later, Kane's left wing was engulfed in the fire, but miraculously neither engine began to burn.

The final seconds before Kane's men reached their release points proved a holocaust of flames and steel. The German flak crews wiped out an entire three-plane flight. One by one, the B-24s fell out of the sky and exploded within the refineries. The last plunged right into a building and blew hunks of masonry and rubble high into the air. Shrapnel tore through the

Teggie Ann, Col. Keith Compton's ride into Ploesti, taxis to the parking area back in Libya following Operation Tidal Wave. Compton's 376th Bomb Group led the entire strike force, but a navigational error sent the Liberandos on a bombing run toward Bucharest, not Ploesti. Compton corrected the mistake, but was forced to make an improvised bomb run on the correct targets from a different direction, which crossed paths with the other groups right when the Americans were most heavily engaged by the German air defense network.

Dedicated ground crews put the final touches on their aircraft in the dark prior to the take-off.

The Liberandos return. For most of the raid's survivors, August 1, 1943, became the seminal moment of their lives. The price of the raid did not just include the physical losses manifested by the empty seats around the chow tent tables that evening. What happened over Southeastern Europe that day would linger in their memories and nightmares for decades to come.

fuselage of another 98th Liberator, wounding three of its crewmen as they fought back with their .50-caliber machine guns.

The survivors completed their runs, dropped their bombs, and sped after Colonel Kane as he led the remains of his command south for home. Even then they were not safe. Fighters made swift, deadly passes on them. Exhausted, the crews fought back, draining the last of their ammunition as they struggled to fend off the Messerschmitts and Romanian IAR-80s. Several more Pyramiders went down.

Ultimately, of the thirty-eight B-24s Colonel Kane led into the target area, only twelve made it back to Libya. Five diverted to fields in Sicily or Cyprus, too battled damaged to make it across the Med. The flak and fighters the group faced destroyed eighteen B-24s with almost 180 men aboard.

The 44th, 93rd, and 389th waded into the fray, B-24s criss-crossing paths in the mad scramble to get to their assigned targets. Wave after wave of Liberators dodged smoke stacks, ducked low behind terrain features to avoid anti-aircraft fire, and braved the ocean of flames

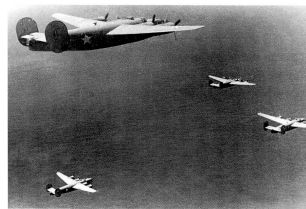

B-24s over the Mediterranean. The Ploesti raid required the crews to navigate at low altitude for 2,700 miles. Some of the Liberators were airborne for over fifteen hours, a grueling psychological and physical challenge for the young air crews.

A wave of Liberators enters the Ploesti inferno. Facing flak, fighters, geysers of flame, debris, and exploding delayed-action bombs dropped by preceding waves, the losses over the target area were appalling.

Colonel John "Killer" Kane, commander of the 98th Bomb Group. During the height of the attack, he led his Pyramiders into the fray even as flak trains shot up his formations. Of the thirty-six Liberators he took into the flames of Ploesti, only twelve reached Libya after the mission. For his valor and stubborn determination, Colonel Kane received the Medal of Honor.

now boiling from the refineries. The 93rd lost two of its B-24s to a midair collision as they came off the bomb run. Another nine more Libs from the Traveling Circus went down. The 389th lost six of its twenty-nine B-24s, and the 44th returned home less eleven of its thirty-eight aircraft. Out of sheer desperation, some of the crews dragged their battered B-24s to Turkey, where they crash-landed. The Turkish authorities interned the surviving crew members.

Altogether, the five groups lost 54 out of the 164 Liberators that made it to the target area, a loss rate of 32 percent. Most of the remaining bombers that did get back to friendly bases had suffered major damage during the running battle over the Balkans. Of the 1,751 air crew on the mission, 306 were killed, 139 captured, 69 interned in Turkey, and 4 escaped and evaded, returning to Allied territory in the months that followed. Many more crewmen returned to Libya, their bodies torn by shrapnel and bullets. The one mission had virtually destroyed the Ninth Air Force's strategic bombing capabilities.

The Germans lost about a hundred anti-aircraft gunners. Two Luftwaffe pilots and three Romanian pilots were killed intercepting the B-24s.

For the American survivors, there was no time to rest. Brereton sent them up against targets in Italy the very next day. What aluminum could withstand, flesh would be tested to the utmost. The campaign would continue with ruthless execution.

And what of Ploesti? Post-strike reconnaissance missions returned with photos that showed the crews had performed extraordinarily in the face of so much opposition. Much

An onrushing, if ragged and battle-thinned, wave of B-24s on the bomb run over Ploesti.

The oil refineries were equipped with smoke generators designed to obscure them from high-level bombers. Here, the white smoke from them mingles with billowing black clouds boiling up from burning oil tanks.

Operation Tidal Wave was the first and only time strategic bombers were used on the deck in the European Theater. Hoping to maximize accuracy and minimize detection, the nap-of-the-earth flying also made the Liberators easy targets for the three hundred anti-artillery guns defending Ploesti. Here, a formation of B-24s hugs the earth as it speeds to the release point.

A reconnaissance photo of the Standard Oil Refinery at Ploesti. It was not seriously damaged during the attack, something the Nazi propaganda machine was quick to point out and note that both the French and British-sponsored refineries had been hammered.

of refinery facilities had been devastated, though the strike missed the one American-built plant owned by Standard Oil, a fact that was played up by Axis propaganda. Brereton later claimed that Operation Tidal Wave destroyed 60 percent of Ploesti's output. While that number was high, the damage was extensive.

And yet, Jacob Smart's get rich quick scheme failed to deliver the knock out blow to the Reich's military machine. The reason why was rooted in the nuances of aerial economic warfare. First, when the Liberators reached Ploesti that August, the seven refineries had been operating far below their maximum capacity. Altogether, the seven plants could produce 9.5 million tons of oil. But that summer, the production rate was only 4.75 million tons. In the days following the attack, the Romanian workers busily rerouted production to the unharmed facilities and brought on-line the unused capacity. Within weeks, the black gold of Ploesti flowed from its refineries once again, to be whisked away in rail road tanker cars to feed the Third Reich's voracious appetite for fuel.

Ploesti left both an enduring legacy and a scar on the USAAF. Such heavy losses, when combined with what was to follow over northwest Europe in the weeks to come, finally convinced the senior strategic bombing leadership that the campaign as envisioned in the inter-war period was simply not going to work. Unescorted bombers, no matter how many defensive guns they possessed, could not defend themselves against determined interceptors. It would take several more grievous lessons to hammer that point home, but Ploesti was a turning point in that shift of mindsets.

It was the resolution and courage of the American air crews that left the most enduring legacy. Where other air forces would have turned back in the face of such incredible opposition, men like Col. John Kane pressed the attack and refused to be dissuaded. The courage this required cannot be underestimated. Flying below the treetops, hedgehopping across the Romanian countryside, the pilots clearly saw what they were in for as they approached the swirling inferno over Ploesti. They could not doubt their fate. That their hands remained steady on the controls, their hearts resolved because they believed in the mission's importance, left an example of heroism unsurpassed in American aviation history. Five men, including Colonel Kane, received the Medal of Honor for their valor that day. Their Balaclava-like charge at Ploesti sent a clear message to the Germans: The Americans would not be dissuaded.

The target area during the climax of the attack.

During the initial deep penetration raids over Germany, the bomber gunners discovered they had to watch their ammunition supply carefully. So many fighters would attack their formations that often they'd run out of .50-caliber ammunition. After missions like Regensburg and Schweinfurt, the waist gunners stood in ankle-deep piles of spent brass, a testament to the ferocity of the fighting.

8

THE WHEELS COME OFF

This was to be my 25th mission. I was so battle weary I could hardly function, but I acted. I did what I thought was right. Maybe, subconsciously, I knew it would be over one way or another . . . there were only two of us left from the top squadron.
—*Carl Fyler,* Staying Alive

AUGUST 1943 WAS THE MONTH FOR E-TICKET TARGETS. While Ploesti attracted the Ninth Air Force, the Eighth cast around for something really substantial to bomb. Colonel Richard D'Orly Hughes, VIII Bomber Command's chief targeting officer, studied his maps and reviewed his lists of aircraft factories and their estimated production levels in search of some German Achilles' heel the Americans could exploit. He thought he found that weakness in three locations: Schweinfurt, Regensburg and Wiener Neustadt. The aircraft factories at Regensburg and Wiener Neustadt accounted for almost half the Luftwaffe's fighter production, while Schweinfurt produced half of the Third Reich's ball bearings.

Could a triple strike hammer all of these choice targets at once? Such an operation would require coordinating with the Ninth Air Force in Libya; Wiener Neustadt was located near Vienna, Austria, and was out of the Eighth Air Force's range.

Weather issues conspired against such cooperation. When the skies cleared over Western Europe, they clouded over to the south. The Ninth ended up bombing Wiener Neustadt on its own on August 13, 1943. Using the sixty-five remaining Liberators that survived the inferno of Ploesti, the Ninth surprised the Germans with this deep penetration raid. Hardly any interceptors were based in the area and for a change the B-24 crews didn't take it on the chin. Only a few bombers were lost. The raid failed anyway; the bombardiers missed their targets.

Forts over England. By the summer of 1943, the Eighth Air Force had grown strong enough to attempt deep penetration raids into the Third Reich. The theory of daylight precision bombing would finally be put to the test.

The Messerschmitt Bf-109G was the most common Eighth Air Force adversary over Germany's skies in 1943. Over thirty-five thousand 109s were built during the war. While an excellent air superiority fighter, the 109 was not a particularly good bomber interceptor. It lacked the firepower of the Bf-110 or the Fw-190, a severe disadvantage when attacking the ultra-rugged Flying Fortress.

The Eighth Air Force targeting specialists searched for weak spots in the German war machine and its industrial base, hoping to locate some key facility that when destroyed could materially affect the war right away.

That left the Eighth Air Force to tackle Regensburg and Schweinfurt. VIII Bomber Command concocted a complicated and timing-based plan that required a lot of moving pieces to function without normal operational friction. General Curtis LeMay's 4th Bomb Wing would lead the mission with the elite 96th Bomb Group at the tip of a spear 139 bombers strong. Regensburg would be their target for the day. Located deep inside Germany, LeMay's B-17s would face the ultimate test: could they survive for hours unescorted in the face of determined Luftwaffe interception? To maximize their chances, LeMay came up with a new type of mutually supporting formation that required three bomb groups. He had twelve total under his command, so he organized them into four tightly-drawn "combat wings," each with a middle group, a high group, and a low group flying in close proximity to one another. This way, the groups could cover each other's flanks with their B-17s massed defensive gun power.

The 1st Bomb Wing was supposed to follow directly behind the 4th with a fifteen-minute interval between the two formations. Once over Central Germany, the 1st would veer off to bomb Schweinfurt, hopefully surprising the Luftwaffe's radar operators with the sudden course change.

To further confuse the Luftwaffe, LeMay's men would not turn back for England. Instead, his Forts would continue southward to land in North Africa. This represented the first of several "shuttle" bombing missions performed by the Eighth.

On August 17, 1943—the one-year anniversary of the Mighty Eighth's first mission—weather reconnaissance aircraft detected clear skies over the target areas. In England, however, the crews sat next to their B-17s enduring mist, fog, and light rain. LeMay didn't let that stop him. He'd trained his groups in instrument take-offs, and after a ninety-minute delay, his men gained the sky, formed up into a column some fifteen miles long, and headed for Regensburg.

The Germans attacked them over Belgium. Swarms of interceptors swept out down into deadly head-on passes. The Luftwaffe pilots concentrated on the trailing combat wing—the unlucky 91st again along with the 381st. The escorting American P-47s could not handle the German onslaught, and the interceptors broke through their cordon to flame six of LeMay's B-17s. At the German frontier, the Thunderbolts ran low on fuel and turned for home, leaving the Forts to the depredations of hundreds of German fighters. Before even reaching Regensburg, another eight Forts went spinning down to their destruction.

Bombing from below 20,000 feet, the 4th Wing inflicted considerable damage to the aircraft factories. Later estimates put the production loss at almost a thousand fighters. With their bays now empty, the Forts continued southward for North Africa, a move that did catch the Luftwaffe's ground controllers by surprise. A few Bf-110s gave chase, shooting down three more American planes.

Curtis LeMay (far right) led the 4th Bomb Wing during the famous double strike mission to Regensburg and Schweinfurt. LeMay's combat experience in the Eighth Air Force shaped his vision of strategic bombing for years to come. Later, he commanded the B-29 forces in the Pacific and burned Japan's major cities to the ground. After the war, he forged Strategic Air Command into an elite and highly effective force.

Early in 1943, the Boeing B-17E began to be replaced by the B-17F. This early Fort arrived in England with an unusual camouflage pattern that resembled the standard RAF disruptive scheme.

Meanwhile, the 1st Bomb Wing did not leave its airfields until LeMay's had been in the air for five hours. The delay, caused by the weather in East Anglia, set the table for a catastrophe. Once aloft, the 222 bombers in this second wave managed to place a perfect interval between themselves and LeMay's men—at least from the German perspective. The timing allowed the Luftwaffe's fighters to land, rearm, and refuel. Some of the 109 and Fw-190 pilots even had time to grab a bite to eat before taking to the air again.

The Luftwaffe's ground controllers had spent much of the afternoon marshalling resources to really pound the 4th Wing when it headed back to England. Instead of facing off against the 4th Wing, these interceptors turned out to be perfectly placed to devastate the second American wave.

Some three hundred fighters tore into the 1st Wing's formation. This time, they concentrated on the lead combat box. Seventeen Flying Forts fell out of the sky as the fighters made relentless attacks from all quarters. Over Schweinfurt, the wing had to select a new IP on the fly

A 96th Bomb Group B-17 over Belgium. The 96th was one of the Eighth Air Force's elite outfits, which is why it was selected to lead the Regensburg mission in August 1942.

in order to keep the setting sun out of the eyes of its bombardiers. The last-minute switch threw a monkey wrench into the attack. The crews scattered their bomb loads all over the city.

Fritz Boost, a young Luftwaffe transport pilot, happened to be in Schweinfurt after the raid and saw the damage it inflicted. The bombs had cut neat swatches right through the city, destroying block after block of buildings without causing catastrophic damage to the ball bearings plants located there.

Though production did drop as a result of the attack, the Germans simply made up the shortfall by purchasing ball bearings from the Swedes. Hap Arnold attempted to stop the sale by offering the Swedish government P-51 Mustangs and C-47 Skytrain cargo aircraft, but the Swedes refused the offer and cut a deal with Nazi Germany instead.

Altogether, sixty B-17s failed to return from the Regensburg-Schweinfurt double strike mission. Worse, when LeMay's men reached North Africa, the landing grounds were so primitive that they lacked even basic maintenance facilities. And the 4th Wing's Forts

Boeing could not produce B-17s fast enough to support the global effort against the Axis powers. As a result, construction was contracted to a number of other companies, including Douglas and Vega. This Eighth Air Force B-17 was produced at the Douglas plant in Long Beach, California.

needed a lot of maintenance. Most of the ones that reached North Africa had suffered battle damage. LeMay ended up having to abandon sixty non-flyable B-17s in North Africa. Bombing Regensburg cost the 4th Wing 40 percent of its effective strength.

That night, Bomber Command flattened Peenemünde, Nazi Germany's secret rocket research facility. In the process, Luftwaffe night fighters shot down forty RAF bombers. In one day, the Allied strategic forces had lost a hundred aircraft and close to a thousand men. The staggering losses only grew worse.

After the double strike raid, Eaker began to waver. Did the British have it right after all? He decided to explore the idea of converting the Eighth Air Force to night operations. He sent a squadron from the 305th Bomb Group to the RAF to gain experience in nocturnal raiding.

After a short respite, the Eighth increased its operational tempo through September, reaching an almost fever pitch the following month. The intense losses and the constant missions through the spring and summer had already strained the air crews to the limit of their endurance. Some simply could give no more.

Pilot Bob "Spook" Bender came to England in the spring of 1943 as part of the original cadre of the 95th Bomb Group. During a raid on Lorient, Bender's Fort took a flak hit that knocked out two engines. He dragged the crippled bomber back to England and crashed at the RAF fighter station at Exeter. The B-17 skidded off the runway and took out a highway bridge.

Bender lost two more Forts over the next few missions. Both were so badly shot up by flak and fighters that after he crash-landed back in England they were dragged off for salvage.

On his eighth mission, a raid on the U-boat pens at St. Nazaire, Bender's fourth B-17 took a serious hit that knocked out an engine. This time, they didn't make it home. He and his crew ditched off the French coast and spent most of two days and a night riding the swells in a couple of rubber rafts until a British torpedo boat fished them out of the water.

Eight missions, four crash landings. Psychologically, Bob Bender had given all he had to the strategic bombing cause. While off duty, he went to see a movie with some of his squadron mates. The newsreel that evening featured a piece on the USAAF's bombing campaign and depicted attacks on B-17 formations from Luftwaffe gun camera footage. The sight of the

Two Southerners behind the controls of a B-17. At left is pilot Lt. Bob Boundrecor who hailed from small-town Louisiana. At right is Lt. Ned Hawkins, a native of Jacksonville, Florida.

The crowded confines of a B-17's bomb bay. Sometimes, loading the ordnance could be exceptionally dangerous, and there were cases of bombs exploding. This usually resulted in a lot of casualties.

Forts going down caused Bender to start screaming at his gunners to "Shoot! Shoot!" He ducked behind a balcony railing until his friends eased him out of the building.

A few days later, Bender and his crew went to pick up their fifth B-17. As they took off, he froze at the controls and had to be overpowered. Group sent him to a hospital, where he suffered a complete breakdown. He returned to the States, a psychological casualty who never recovered from his ordeal. At age twenty-five, Bender suffered a fatal heart attack.

The crews just had to put their heads down and endure. They counted their missions and prayed that every briefing would reveal the day's target would be a milk run.

There weren't any milk runs in the fall of 1943.

In October, the 1943 air campaign over Western Europe reached its climax as the Eighth Air Force flew a series of maximum effort strikes deep into Germany. On the eighth, 400 Forts and Liberators returned to Bremen and Vegesack. They returned less 30 bombers and three hundred more airmen. Another 110 limped back to England with battle damage.

The next day, the groups sortied for Germany again, striking Danzig, Marienburg, Anklam and Gdynia with about 350 bombers. Twenty-eight went down while another 150 suffered damage.

The next day, the Eighth flew its third maximum effort mission in three days. Most of

A Luftwaffe Bf-109 pilot with his dog in the cockpit with him. As the 1943 campaign wore on, the average quality of German replacement pilots plummeted.

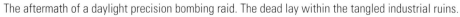
The aftermath of a daylight precision bombing raid. The dead lay within the tangled industrial ruins.

Fritz Boost was a replacement pilot. Trained to fly Messerschmitt Me-323 transports, he was pulled into the Defense of the Reich and taught (briefly) how to fly the Focke-Wulf Fw-190. Fritz had already been shot down on the Eastern Front in a Me-323, ending up in the Black Sea until rescued. Later, as a Focke-Wulf pilot, outnumbered and alone, he was shot down in again in the winter of 1944–1945. After the war, he emigrated to the United States and became a high school teacher.

The end of a Messerschmitt Bf-109, whose surprised pilot did not even have to drop his belly tank.

After the Regensburg raid, LeMay's B-17s reached North Africa in bad shape. Almost 40 percent of his aircraft had either been shot down during the mission or reached North Africa with major damage that grounded them. He had to abandon sixty non-flyable Flying Forts on his return flight to England a few days later.

Tom Paine was a survivor. This B-17 served throughout the war with the 388th Bomb Group and flew countless missions against Nazi Europe only to be scrapped at war's end in June 1945.

Had the Fort not been as durable as it was, the Eighth Air Force's crew losses would have been unsustainable.

General Eaker bore the brunt of the failing long-range penetration effort into Germany. By year's end, he had been bumped to the MTO, never to receive another promotion. He's seen here at war's end as a Soviet official decorates him with a Red Army medal.

the bomber crews had already flown at least one of those, and some had flown on all three. This time, the target was Münster. The Americans ran into a Luftwaffe buzz saw, and within minutes of getting intercepted, the 13th Combat Wing's three groups lost twenty-five planes. The air battle raged all the way to the target and throughout the desperate return to England. Lieutenant John Winant, the son of the American ambassador to Great Britain, was shot down that day while piloting a 390th Group B-17. He managed to bail out and spent the rest of the war in a German POW camp.

This third consecutive deep penetration raid cost the Eighth another thirty bombers and 306 airmen.

Four days later, the Eighth Air Force struck Schweinfurt for the second time. The ball bearings factories proved to be an irresistible lure. This time, the high command held no illusions at how difficult this mission would be on the crews. Word came down from Eighth

The aftermath of an air battle. Spent .50-caliber machine gun rounds rattle around in the bottom of a Flying Fort's fuselage.

Air Force HQ that this target could shorten the war if destroyed. The group commanders received explicit instructions to tell the crews this in hopes that it would motivate them.

Three hundred twenty B-17s and B-24s took off from East Anglia that day. They formed up into their tight combat boxes and drove into the teeth of the Luftwaffe juggernaut. For hours the bomb groups came under fighter attack. Wave after wave of expertly led jagdgeschwaders of Fw-190s and Bf-109s drove their gunnery runs to point-blank range, drilling the American bombers with cannon and machine gun fire. The raid devolved into a parade of slaughter as Fort after Fort went down. Some of the American gunners ran out of

A search and rescue aircraft locates a B-17 that splashed down in the North Sea. A larger boat has been dropped to the crew, who are crammed into a rubber dinghy.

ammunition before reaching the target area, so fierce was the fighting. The B-17 carried about seven thousand rounds for its thirteen machine guns, which gave each crewman only a few minutes of firing time for their weapons.

The 100th Bomb Group suffered the worst that day. After the preceding raids in October, the outfit could only field eight B-17s for the Schweinfurt mission. The Germans cut all eight out of the sky. After that, the unit was known throughout the USAAF as the "Bloody Hundredth."

Once again, Col. Archie Olds and his 96th Bomb Group led the entire force to target aboard a B-17 named *Fertile Myrtle III*. The 96th endured repeated fighter attack for an hour and half on the way to Schweinfurt, but Olds' aircraft evaded damage. During the bomb run, their luck evaporated. A flak shell burst next to the bomber's nose, sending shrapnel into the bombardier's head and legs. Despite his wounds, he crawled back to his Norden sight and laid his bombs on target.

On the way home, the 96th passed over Reims, where a surprise volley of anti-aircraft fire hit *Fertile Myrtle III* a second time. The group's navigator died instantly as shrapnel tore through his back. The bombardier suffered a thigh wound. Olds was blown out of his seat at the same time more shrapnel scythed through the cockpit, wounding two more crewmen. With two engines out, the B-17 entered a dive from 20,000 feet. Somehow, they stayed aloft long enough to get back home and execute an emergency landing. As Olds watched the ground crew remove the bloody remains of the navigator, he said, "Save me a pew in church on Sunday."

The second Schweinfurt raid cost the Eighth Air Force sixty-seven bombers and almost 650 airmen. The 305th Bomb Group incurred 130 of those casualties, a figure that represented 87 percent of the group's strength that day. The 306th lost another 100.

The threat of a forced landing in the North Sea or the English Channel was ever present for the Eighth Air Force crews. In East Anglia, the airmen used cast-off or cannibalized wrecks to train for such a possibility.

Shrapnel wounds from bursting anti-aircraft shells inflicted thousands of casualties on American bomber crews. To protect themselves, the men often wore armor plating, some of which was standard issue. Some airmen had the ground crews fabricate custom armored slabs and even codpieces as well.

Often, the bombs would find their mark and destroy much of a factory complex's structures. Inside, often the vital machine tools, equipment, and generators would survive the onslaught, which allowed the workers to clear debris and get the plant up and running quite quickly.

A waist gunner in action. This was the coldest position in a B-17. With the side windows open to the outside, the temperatures could be as low as sixty below during winter flying at 20,000 feet. Taking gloves off, even for a few seconds, often resulted in frostbite.

In the nose of a B-17F, modified with a pair of .50-caliber machine guns. The bombardier position was not well suited for larger men.

In return, the ball bearing plants took severe damage. Yet, the raid failed to affect the German war machine as hoped. The Third Reich actually possessed a large surplus of ball bearings in the fall of 1943, and whatever more they needed the Swedes readily provided.

Besides, the workers quickly went to work restoring their factories to functioning levels again and within a short time the production rate climbed to pre-attack levels. This represented a major oversight on the part of the prewar strategic bombing advocates. Everyone from Douhet to Trenchard, Spaatz and Mitchell failed to consider that once bombed, a factory could be rebuilt. The Eighth Air Force found itself faced with a multi-dimensional adversary.

Above: Ten Knights in a Bar Room, a 94th Bomb Group B-17G, ran afoul of a Luftwaffe Messerschmitt Bf-110 flown by Lt. Jacob Schaus of Nachtjagdgeschwader-4 during a mission to Emden on October 4, 1943. Schaus shot the bomber down, but all ten men managed to get out of their doomed Fort safely. Three became POWs, and the other seven somehow miraculously evaded capture and returned safely to Allied hands.

Left: The 100th Bomb Group earned a reputation as a jinxed unit. During the October Schweinfurt raid, the entire group was shot down. Throughout much of 1943, the Luftwaffe singled out the group and inflicted severe casualties, prompting many rumors and speculation as to why the 100th seemed to receive such treatment so frequently.

A formation of "Bloody Hundredth" B-17s during a mission in the summer of 1943. One rumor that circulated through the Eighth Air Force explained why the Luftwaffe seemed bent on that group's destruction. During a raid in early 1943, the rumor said, the 100th had machine gunned a German pilot in his parachute after he'd bailed out of his burning interceptor. Word spread through the Defense of the Reich units and the 100th became a marked bomb group. Postwar research failed to confirm any of this. More likely, the 100th flew a looser formation than the other units in its combat wing. The Germans picked up on this and exploited that mistake with relentlessness that led to the deaths of hundreds of American crews.

Me and My Gal, a 384th Bomb Group B-17, became another victim of the Luftwaffe's heavy fighters that fall. A Ju-88 flown by Uffz. Benno Gramlich caught *Me and My Gal* over Simmershofen, Germany, during the October 14, 1943, mission and brought it down. Until the Eighth could protect its bombers from the Luftwaffe's twin engine fighters, deep penetration raids were simply too costly to continue.

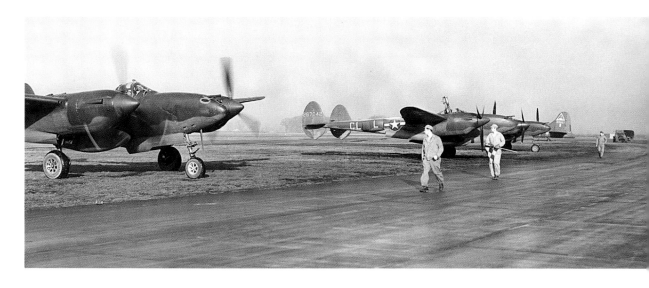

Fifty-fifth Fighter Group P-38 Lightnings on the flight line in England. Though a war-winner in the Southwest Pacific, the P-38 never achieved the same level of success in Northwest Europe against the Luftwaffe, leading to its general replacement with P-51 Mustangs throughout the Eighth Air Force.

Alabama Exterminator II, a 384th Bomb Group B-17, is examined by curious RAF personnel.

All business in a B-17's waist.

Mission debriefing. Landing back in England did not end the day for the Eighth Air Force crews. After securing their bomber, they would gather to go over the details of the mission with their group's intelligence section.

Not only did the bombers have to fight their way through flak and fighters to reach the target areas, but they had to contend with the workers on the ground who patched up the damage their bombs inflicted.

This meant there would be no knock-out blow, no get rich quick target that could shorten the war or bring the Third Reich to its knees. Instead, the USAAF faced the prospect of a grueling, prolonged campaign to not only knock out their targets, but keep them non-operational with repeated attacks.

Schweinfurt underscored the problem with that reality: the Eighth Air Force simply could not absorb the losses such sustained bombing would require. Unescorted strikes deep inside Germany had failed dramatically and at a terrible cost. It was either time to throw in the towel and join the RAF's night campaign or come up with something else that could keep the bomber losses manageable.

It was the something else that saved daylight bombing.

Awaiting the start of a briefing for a mission to Leipzig at the 385th Bomb Group's base at Great Ashfield.

9

THE MORTAL ONES

★ ★ ★ ★ ★

Fred Derry shook his head and walked a path
From bathroom to dresser . . .
Stopped a while and leaned his elbows . . .
Looked against the glass
And saw the snapshots curling there:
The faces of the 305th.
And some were ringed—
He'd put an inky ring around the ones
He'd seen exploded, frying, going down.
—MacKinlay Kantor, Glory For Me

LONG BEFORE SUNRISE, the duty officer awoke the crews for the day's mission, moving from barracks to barracks with a flashlight and a list of names. Groggy, weary men, barely removed from frat parties and family farms, arose in the damp velvet darkness of England at war. A shower and shave in cold water followed an indifferent breakfast: powdered eggs, spam, and coffee thick as syrup. The banter would be forced; uncertainty dominated the mess hall. Where were they going today? Would it be a milk run to the French coast? Or would it be a meat grinder like Schweinfurt or Leipzig, Berlin or Bremen? To the men who would soon mount up in the aluminum depths of their Liberators and Forts, the fickleness of their lot seemed both cruel and capricious. The decisions made above them at wing or command HQ held little reason, only dread thinly concealed with crude jokes and camaraderie.

Breakfast finished, the officers departed for their briefing. It was here that the suspense would be lifted. They sat in wooden

The men of the 305th. Fred Derry was the main character in MacKinlay Kantor's poetic novel, *Glory For Me*, which was written just after the end of the war. Instead of creating a fictional unit for Derry to have flown with while in the Eighth Air Force, Kantor went for added realism and used an actual unit. *Glory For Me* became the basis of the enduring classic film *The Best Years of Our Lives*, which probed the effects of combat on three veterans after they returned home from the war.

Inside the 385th's briefing room. At the back of the room, behind the table and chairs, is a screen for projecting slides and film. It was here that the crews assigned to the day's mission would learn the target they were to bomb.

Once the group commander announced the target for the day, the intelligence officer would usually walk through the planned mission in detail, using a huge wall map of Europe to illustrate the critical elements of the raid.

Course to the target was usually denoted by a red ribbon or string. The longer it stretched into Nazi-held Europe, the more groans and sounds of angst would arise from the audience.

chairs clad in their A-2 flight jackets, boots and khaki pants, waiting for the group commander to stride into the room and stand before his men. Elmer Bendiner wrote of this daily ritual in *The Fall of the Fortresses*: "We sat as if in school assembly. The death's-head-and-crossed-bombs insignia on our leather jackets and the pistols dangling from our belts lent a boyish wickedness to the scene."

When the commander arrived, the room went silent and the tension immediately spiked. Behind their old-man facades, these boy-warriors prayed for an easy mission. The daily toll of deep strikes had left them weary. The strategic air war had become a test of human endurance, and all had known men whose character could not withstand this test. They failed in odd and sometimes dramatic ways. Those who kept slogging aged well beyond their tender years as friends died or came home in shattered blood-stained bombers, their bodies burned, torn or disfigured by shrapnel and bullets.

They'd long since learned that the glory they saw back home on small town silver screens simply did not exist in the skies over Germany. Physically and psychologically, the strategic bombing campaign was a death march that only the luckiest and strongest would survive.

The group commander would make a few introductory comments. Perhaps he'd crack a joke to ease the tension. But then, it was down to business. "The target for today is . . ."

For America, the strategic bombing campaign may have been planned in the prewar era by professional USAAF officers, but it was carried out by average young men from all walks of life, most of whom had never set foot in an airplane prior to the Pearl Harbor attack.

Behind him, a map would be concealed until this moment. Operational security was taken very seriously, so the mission's destination would remain a closely guarded secret for as long as possible.

The map would reveal relief or angst. The officers seated in those wooden chairs cheered or groaned as they greeted the news. Milk run or flak trap. Fighter escort, or go it alone. Colored lines denoted the ingress and egress routes. The time hacks each squadron would be required to meet were carefully reviewed and noted.

At times, the mission requirements left some of the men in attendance with greatly troubled hearts. These were young Americans, steeped in the traditions of their family's

For some of the air crews, the campaign against Germany elicited moral concerns. Massive bombing of cities, cloaked in terms like "precision bombardment" could not help but produce massive civilian casualties. To some of these young men, this was an extremely difficult mission to carry out.

The Münster raid broke from the doctrine of precision bombing on industrial targets. For the first time, the Eighth Air Force deliberately placed a civilian workforce in the Norden's crosshairs. Here, the 94th Bomb Group plods its way to the target area, where 30 out of the 236 bombers that reached the target would be lost. Four days later, the Eighth Air Force launched the famous double strike raid on Schweinfurt and Regensburg, culminating what became known as Black Week. Today, the United States officially celebrates this grim period in aerial history with National Eighth Air Force week, October 8–14.

religion. Had not Pearl Harbor been savaged in a surprise attack, most would have passed their years in ordinary anonymity devoid of violence or unnatural death. Instead, circumstance led them to this place where they were expected to kill their enemies without question or remorse. For some, the philosophical or spiritual beliefs they cherished conflicted with their duty at hand.

In one early case, the Eighth Air Force laid on a strike against Münster, a key choke point in the industrial Ruhr Valley's railroad network. The target stripped away any pretense of precision, pinpoint bombing designed to minimize civilian casualties. Rather, the Münster raid's purpose was the very opposite. Time over target was picked to be the moment church got out on a Sunday morning in October 1943. The medieval cathedral in the heart of the city was designated as the aiming point. Eighth Bomber command wanted to kill as many employees of the nearby railroad marshalling yard as possible, thus hindering attempts to repair the tracks, a fact that was briefed to the B-17 crews of the 95th Bomb Group the morning of the raid.

In the predawn hours before a mission, final preparations are made on a 91st Bomb Group B-17G.

After the officers completed the morning briefing, they rejoined the rest of their crew and pushed down all the relevant information to them. Not long after this photo was taken, the 381st Bomb Group B-17G *Button Nose* took a flak hit over Caen on August 8, 1944, and went down in flames.

Shrouded in fog, a B-17 awaits its crew at Bassingbourn. Ground fog played havoc with the bomber groups during take-off. Forming up in this sort of thick soup was also quite dangerous and led to many aerial collisions.

Sitting in the audience that day was the 95th's lead navigator, Capt. Ellis Scripture. In Ian Hawkins' excellent work, *The Münster Raid*, Scripture remarked:

> I'd been raised in a strict Protestant home. I was shocked to learn that we were to bomb civilians as our primary target . . . and that our aiming point was to be the front steps of the Münster Cathedral at noon on Sunday, just as Mass was completed. I was very reluctant to fly this mission.

Scripture's qualms were in the distinct minority. Most of the aircrews settled into their grim and violent jobs and did as they were told. In this war, the gloves had come off a long time ago, and every mission they found themselves in a bare knuckled brawl with the best interceptor pilots the world had ever seen. After experiencing that, charity and mercy became early casualties.

After the group commander and his intelligence officer briefed the final mission details, the men dispersed to go brief the rest of their crews. The enlisted men and NCOs who formed the majority of each bomber's human complement would be found killing time

playing poker or reading, or writing a final letter home. Anxiously, they crowded around their pilot, who served as the plane captain and was responsible for all of them. In these minutes, the pilot pushed down the information his crew would need to execute the mission. Once that was done, the men would settle in to wait for the go-order.

That wait could grow interminable, thanks to the European weather. Reconnaissance planes over the target area transmitted last-minute details back to England, including updated weather reports. Many times the target might be clear, but the airfields in East Anglia or the Foggia Plain would be blanketed with fog. Other times, the fields were clear but the targets were obscured. Prewar strategists had never seriously considered something as mundane as

The crew of a Fifteenth Air Force B-24 arrives for the preflight check and routine.

Waiting for the go-order was always tension filled and difficult.

weather into their conceptualized bombing campaigns. Here on the front lines, it served as one of the great limiting factors on what the bombers could actually achieve. Missions were scrubbed almost every week thanks to storms over the home airfields or cloud cover over the target area. Come fall and winter, clear skies grew increasingly rare. Snowbound bombers sat in their revetments, the air war on hold thanks to the power of Mother Nature.

On most days, the crews assembled and drove out to the flight line to their assigned bombers. The Army Air Forces took a lenient attitude toward individualizing aircraft, and the crews took advantage of that. The talented artists in each group painted artwork on the nose, while the crew or pilot selected a name for their aircraft. Away from home, restraint and taste frequently did not factor into the name or the artwork. Naked women abounded, buttressed by dirty names and ribald humor. In some cases, the aircraft's name mirrored the type of humor, music, or entertainment the crew enjoyed. In fact, nose art and plane names served as a wellspring of sociological information about the men who flew the bombers.

The customization did not stop with the name or the nose art. The gunners, navigators, and other crewmen frequently added their own touches on the fuselage around their position. A

Opposite: Nose art ranged from the sublime to the raunchy and serves as a window into the sociological climate of the USAAF during World War II. Lesser known than nose art is the personal additions other crew members, both ground and air, made to their bombers.

Inside the bombers, the group's armorers had already cleaned, oiled, and installed the defensive weapons and filled the ready ammunition boxes with as much lead and brass as they could hold.

motto, a name that meant something to the man behind the weapon, or swastikas representing interceptors downed and aerial firefights won gave these men a greater sense of ownership in their aircraft.

The pre-mission checklists were long. As the briefed take-off time approached, the crews would work through their lists. The ground crews had already done much of the work. The machine guns were cleaned, oiled, and installed. Ready ammunition for each position had been placed inside their aircraft. The bombs to be dropped that day already sat snug in the bomb bays.

Once the work was done, the checklists reviewed, the men settled down to wait once again. If weather delayed the mission, this could be the worst time of all, especially if the

target was a tough one. Idle time meant time for the brain to engage and think about what was soon to come. And yet, uncertainty often persisted. Would weather delay the mission or scrub it altogether? They hung on tidbits of information passed along from crew to crew as they sat with their gear in the damp grass beside their planes. Not a few threw up as the tension manifested physically in them.

The lack of control over one's own fate was among the most difficult psychological aspects of the strategic air war. A crew could perform their functions flawlessly and still be blown out of the sky by flak or fighters. A random anti-aircraft shell, fired from five miles below by an illiterate conscript could kill a dozen Americans in an eye blink. A mechanical

When the bomb groups received the go-order and the mission began, Wright Cyclone engines and Pratt & Whitneys roared to life. Hundreds of them merged together to create a unique sound that resonated for miles across the countryside.

The sheer randomness of who lived and who died created a unique dynamic within the ranks of the strategic bomber crews. That sense of helplessness and inability to control their fate caused many of the men to become superstitious. Comfort was found in rituals and routines considered "lucky," and many of the men carried small talisman with them into the air. Such behavior served as a psychological safety valve.

failure could cripple the unlucky bomber and force it out of formation, leaving it terribly vulnerable to the predacious interceptors that thrived on such easy pickings.

That sense of helplessness created a whole subculture of superstition. If one routine worked and the crew returned home, it would be duplicated for every mission thereafter. The men clung to lucky charms and placed their faith in a higher power. In a 1984 NBC documentary called *All the Fine Young Men*, Elmer Bendiner recalled:

> We resorted to magic . . . you pick up talisman. If you do one thing and you come home that night, well that's the thing to do. Whether it's the way you tie your scarf around your neck or the socks you put on your feet. It's a kind of do-it-yourself superstition— you make it up as you go.

The veterans had long since ritualized their routines. The new crews, the replacements who'd never encountered such tension or psychological pressure, learned from the old hands. If they survived.

The go-order roused the men to their feet. The savvy ones emptied their bladders right there around the aircraft, for the missions could last upwards of ten hours as their groups plodded across Europe at 170 miles an hour. One by one, they swung themselves through the forward hatch or climbed into the bomb bays to take up their assigned stations.

Engines turned over. The ground shook as the big radials roared to life. One bomb group typically included over a hundred engines, and they could be heard starting up for miles across the English and Italian countryside. The locals living nearby always knew a mission was on when the ground began to shake and windows rattled in their frames. Frequently, on Sunday mornings, the civilians would fill the pews in the local churches, and the sudden cacophony of the Pratt & Whitneys would drown out the pastor's service.

Back at the fields, the danger began. From the moment the chocks were pulled away from the main wheels, the risk of death or grievous wound came from a myriad of sources. Just taxiing to the runway could be dangerous, especially in foggy conditions. Ground collisions between B-24s and B-17s were not uncommon. Such calamities often led to mass casualty events right there at the home station as fuel burned and bombs cooked off in the wake of such accidents.

Taking off was the next gut-check moment. The crews were taught to launch thirty seconds apart. Often, this was achieved either in fog or in pre-dawn darkness. If a fully loaded bomber

With the engines started, the bombers would then taxi to the runways. From this moment on, the potential dangers and chance of sudden death were many and varied.

The 381st Bomb Group lines up for take-off. In such a crowded environment, catastrophic accidents were depressingly common.

Collisions on the ground while taxiing claimed many aircraft and lives. Here, a pair of 401st Bomb Group B-17s ran into each other in the typically foggy morning conditions in England.

Two fatal accidents. When loaded with fuel, bombs, and ammunition, the bombers were explosive tinder boxes, terribly vulnerable to destruction should something go wrong on the runways during take-off.

To make it easier for the pilots to find their groups amid the aerial chaos over Southern Italy or East Anglia, the USAAF developed garishly painted and easily identifiable "circus ships" that were used as aerial rally points for the groups to use as they linked up after take-off. They represent some of the most outlandish paint schemes ever employed by American aircraft.

The finished product: Formed up and ready to go, the 381st Bomb Group heads east toward the hostile skies of Nazi-held Europe.

crashed as it sped down the field, sometimes the aircraft behind it would not know it. They'd begin their take-off rolls only to drive right into the flaming ruins of the preceding bomber.

Once airborne, the risk of collision actually increased. Forming up by squadrons and groups into the tight combat boxes took time, skill and precision. Again, the weather often played havoc with such a delicate operation. To make things easier for the pilots, each group used a "circus ship" to help assemble their formations. Usually, these were outdated or war-weary B-24s or B-17s that had been painted in garish, easily recognizable ways. That way in the crowded skies over England and Italy, the men could tack on to their circus ship as it orbited. Once assembled, the squadron and groups would then merge with their neighbors until finally the entire wing had formed up. The gunners would test fire their weapons over the Channel or North Sea, the pilots would concentrate on staying tucked in tight as their flights bounced and bucked in turbulence and prop wash. The North Sea and the Channel served almost as the strategic war's no-mans-land. They represented the last stretch of real estate not dominated by the Third Reich. Once the coast appeared, the battle would be joined. It was time to meet the enemy.

A Mustang I running low over the European countryside. The RAF tactical reconnaissance squadrons relied on hedge-hopping and speed to avoid detection, interception, and anti-aircraft fire. The photos they brought back helped shape the D-Day invasion plan.

10

THE HYBRID STALLION

"When I saw Mustangs over Berlin, I knew the war was lost."
—Hermann Goering

DROP TANKS, FUEL MANAGEMENT, and a new fighter saved the daylight strategic bombing campaign. Ironically, all three solutions found their way to Europe despite entrenched resistance from the USAAF's stateside bureaucracy.

Drop tanks—external fuel cells that could be released after the gas inside them had been consumed—had been around for several years. The Germans had them available for their Bf-109s during the Battle of Britain but failed to employ them as well. Basically, what it came down to was this: hanging stuff under a fleet-of-foot fighter made them far less fleet-of-foot, and that was anathema to the fighter purists within the USAAF.

Fortunately, there are always rebels in uniform willing to buck the establishment and do what is right, not what is acceptable or career-friendly. Colonel Cass Hough was one of those brilliant rogues. Before the war, he'd been the CEO of the Daisy Air Rifle Company and had made millions selling BB guns to an entire generation of American kids. He possessed a sharp intellect, courage, and a solid understanding of engineering. As a pilot himself, he also grasped many of the issues facing the combat crews in England.

During the war, as the commander of the Eighth Air Force's Technical Service Section, he watched the bombers come home shot full of holes day after day and began to ponder how he could extend the range of the existing fighters serving in England. The Spitfire was never going to be more than a short-range air superiority

Designed and built in less than four months, the North American Mustang was the product of a British need for more fighters. Originally, the RAF simply wanted North American to build Curtiss P-40s for it. The management at North American believed they could do better—and they did.

The USAAF took an interest in the new North American design and ordered fighter, reconnaissance, and dive-bomber versions of it.

weapon. The P-47 was a different story. In 1943, on internal fuel, the Thunderbolt pilots could hang with the bombers for about 230 miles before they had to turn back.

Hough experimented with existing American ferry tanks at first. He found them lacking in every respect. At altitude, some would not feed properly. Others banged against the underside of the fuselage or wing, even at normal cruising speeds. The lightweight paper tanks tended to leak after only a few hours.

Hough realized he needed a new design. He looked at British auxiliary tanks, then settled on fabricating his own. Since the fighters operated above 20,000 feet most of the time, the tanks had to be pressurized in order to feed properly at such heights. That proved to be a tricky engineering problem. Nevertheless, by May 1943, he and his men developed a steel-fabricated hundred-gallon tank for the P-47. Once approved, the design was contracted to local British firms, but a shortage of sheet metal hampered production through the summer.

Hough looked for another alternative. He began playing around with a British 108-gallon ferry tank made out of paper. With some finesse, his engineers came up with a way to

The dive-bomber variant of the Mustang was designated the A-36. It served in the Mediterranean and China-Burma-India theaters.

The Mustang I probably would have been relegated to an aviation history footnote had it not been for Ronald Harker, Rolls-Royce's chief test pilot. He flew one and realized that if the Allison engine could be replaced with a Rolls-Royce Merlin, the Mustang's performance and range would be significantly enhanced. He advocated such an experiment despite red tape and bureaucratic opposition. The result was a hybrid Anglo-American effort that would play a significant part in winning the war.

strengthen the tanks so that they could withstand pressurization. The new version went into production in July 1943.

A shortage of drop tanks marred the summer and fall. In desperation, some four thousand seventy-five-gallon cells designed for the P-39 arrived in England. The fighter groups put them to good use until the larger tanks became available in sufficient numbers. Through the fall, larger tanks went into production, and the P-47 was modified to be able to carry them under the wings as well as the fuselage centerline.

A P-51A at a depot in England. It would not be until the marriage between American airframe and British engine that the Mustang became a world-class fighter. Even then, its significance to the strategic bombing campaign was totally missed by the Eighth Air Force's leadership until Jimmy Doolittle arrived to replace Eaker in early 1944.

An early Mustang undergoing cold-weather testing in Alaska.

By early 1944, the Thunderbolt units could carry aloft an extra three hundred gallons of fuel under their wings. This gave the Jug pilots the legs to stretch deep into the Third Reich. Given that the P-47 composed the majority of the VIII Fighter Command's available strength, extending their radius of action played the single most important role in winning the air war in 1944.

At the same time the tanks came into widespread use, the USAAF underwent a mini-revolution in fuel management, thanks in part to Charles Lindbergh. The famed aviator traveled all over the world, showing American pilots that if they leaned out their fuel mixtures, raised their manifold pressure in their engines, and slowed the revolutions per minute their propellers made, they could significantly extend their radius of action. The P-38 pilots went from being able to spend four or five hours in the air to eight to ten—longer by war's end with the addition of larger external tanks. Inevitably, the Jug pilot's of the 56th Fighter Group made it all the way to Berlin and back on more than one occasion before the war ended in May 1945.

Drop tanks and fuel management never received the press they deserved for saving the daylight strategic bombing campaign. Instead, the Mustang absorbed most of that credit. Born from a British design requirement, turned into the USAAF's only dedicated single-seat dive bomber used during the war, the Mustang eventually morphed into history's ultimate long-range air superiority weapon.

In 1940, the British came to the United States on an aviation shopping spree. Desperate for aircraft to use against the Germans and knowing that their own production capacity was very limited, the British Purchasing Commission traveled around America offering contracts for such planes as the Curtiss P-40 and the Lockheed Hudson. When the Brits reached North American Aviation, they asked the company to build P-40s under license for the RAF. That did not appeal to North American's management, and instead the company offered to build a totally new fighter design that incorporated all the hard-won lessons learned in Europe so far. What's more, they promised to build the prototype in 120 days.

The British agreed and the race was on. North American put the project in full gear and made everyone work sixteen hour days, seven days a week. The effort paid off: after 117 days, the prototype rolled out of the factory. Dubbed the XNA-73, the new fighter used a 1,100-horsepower Allison engine as its power plant. Test flights encouraged the British so much that they ordered it into production. The first Mustang I, as the RAF called it, took flight in April 1941. At low altitudes, it could beat anything in the air, including the Spitfire. Below 10,000 feet, it could best a Spitfire's top speed by thirty-five miles an hour.

Further flight evaluations in 1941 and early 1942, however, demonstrated a serious lack of power above 15,000 feet. The Allison engine without a supercharger just could not perform at altitude. Fighter Command rejected the new aircraft, and it was sent to the purgatory of army cooperation and reconnaissance squadrons, where they went into operational service starting in the spring of 1942.

The USAAF took notice of the new design as well. When North American adapted the Mustang to the dive bombing role, the Army ordered five hundred of them. Called the A-36

An A-36 over Mount Vesuvius. The A-36 filled the dive-bombing role quite well, though by the time it arrived such tactics had fallen out of favor within the USAAF.

P-51A Mustangs served in combat in the China-Burma-India Theater, where they gained a reputation as excellent fighter-bombers.

The 31st Fighter Group left England in 1942 to take part in the North African campaign. The outfit never returned to the Eighth Air Force. Instead, it joined the XIV Fighter Command when it was activated at the end of 1943. Re-equipped with Mustangs, the 31st provided long-range escort for the Liberators and Forts of the XIV for the rest of the war.

Invader, they would see combat in the Mediterranean with both ground attack units and reconnaissance squadrons.

Later, the USAAF ordered a fighter variant as well, which originally was called the P-51A Apache. They saw service in the China-Burma-India Theater and the Mediterranean.

In April 1942, Ronald Harker, the chief test pilot for Britain's Rolls-Royce's aircraft engine department, flew to Duxford and climbed into a Mustang I's cockpit for the first time. A man of vision and great energy, he quickly saw the Mustang's potential. He noted that the new plane could carry three times the fuel the Spitfire could, and then he wondered what might happen if the airframe was mated to a Rolls-Royce Merlin engine. The Merlins tended to sip less fuel than the gas-hungry Allison, and the idea of such a union intrigued him enough that he went to his superiors to advocate for such an experiment.

He came up against a lot of opposition and RAF disinterest in the American design, but he stuck with his idea until he finally got approval. The test showed it to be a match made in heaven,

The P-51B quickly showed its mastery over the Bf-109 and Fw-190A. Initially armed with four .50-caliber machine guns, the new fighter did suffer from frequent weapon jams. It only took a few months to fix that problem, and after that the Mustang came into its own just in time to help deliver the knock-out blow to the Luftwaffe.

perhaps the best example of trans-Atlantic technical cross-pollination during the entire war. The new Merlin-powered aircraft excited everyone. Back in the States, North American saw it as a chance to save the design, and the high-altitude, long-range performance the new engine offered gave it considerable potential. Hap Arnold quickly grasped that and ordered over two thousand in late 1942.

To keep pace with the airframe's production, Packard was given a contract to build the Merlin under license in the United States. By November 1942 the first Packard/Merlin P-51 rolled off the assembly line at North American's Inglewood plant in Southern California.

Known as the P-51B Mustang, the aircraft replaced the 354th Fighter Group's aging P-39 Airacobras during the final phases of that outfit's pre-deployment work up in the United States. In December 1943, the "Pioneer Mustangs" reached England and joined, ironically, the Ninth Air Force, which was a dedicated tactical aviation organization.

It didn't matter. The 354th Fighter Group began flying long-range escort missions with the Eighth Air Force almost immediately. When married to long-range drop tanks, the new Mustangs could range the length and breadth of the Third Reich. No longer would the Forts and Libs be left alone to face hordes of Luftwaffe interceptors. The only thing the Americans

Max Lamb, one of the 354th Fighter Group's aces, sits in the cockpit of his P-51. The Pioneer Mustangs produced no fewer than forty-five aces during its amazing combat career.

Lieutenant William Groceclose climbs out of his 4th Fighter Group P-51. The 4th earned fame as the top-scoring Eighth Air Force unit during the war, accounting for over a thousand Luftwaffe aircraft on the ground and in the air.

Armorers prepare to load .50-caliber ammunition into the wings of a 4th Fighter Group P-51. The D model carried six guns instead of the earlier variants' four.

The "Bottisham Four"—a legendary quartet of 361st Fighter Group P-51 Mustangs led by Thomas Christian's *Lou IV.* Christian, a West Point graduate, was only twenty-eight years old when he was killed in August 1944. This photo was part of a series shot from a 91st Bomb Group B-17 on July 26, 1944.

Big Friend, Little Friend. The Mustang saved countless bomber crews and ensured the success of the 1944 strategic bombing campaign.

Lieutenant Colonel Thomas Christian flies over England in August 1944. Christian lived only a few more days after this photo was taken. He was killed in combat on August 12, 1944.

Don Blakeslee, legendary fighter leader, tactician, and ace, commanded the 4th Fighter Group. He had flown with one of the RAF's Eagle Squadrons prior to the U.S. entry in the war, and in the years that followed he flew more missions and accumulated more combat hours than just about any other fighter pilot in the European Theater.

A formation of 361st Fighter Group P-51D Mustangs in flight over England late in the war. The D model arrived in theater later in 1944 sporting a new canopy that provided much better all-round visibility than did the B and C razorback versions.

needed now was more Mustang groups. Through the first months of 1944, new ones arrived nearly every week. The famed 4th Fighter Group turned in their P-47s and took delivery of factory-fresh Mustangs. Most of its pilots had served with the Eagle Squadrons in the RAF and had loved their graceful Spitfires and never liked their heavier, less maneuverable Jugs. But when they climbed into their new Mustangs, they knew they'd been given a true thoroughbred—one that would take them to Berlin and back.

The end of 1943 saw the confluence of these developments reach England just in the nick of time to save the daylight bombing campaign. It was true serendipity and set the stage for the massive air battles that determined the fate of the Third Reich in the ensuing six months. Without the fuel tanks, without the Mustang, the Eighth Air Force's campaign would have remained dead in the water. Now, as 1944 began, the Eighth would return to the skies over Germany with renewed energy, a new mission, and fighter escort needed to get the job done.

361st Fighter Squadron P-51 ace Vernon Richards. He flew a Mustang named *Tika IV*. The 361st, 352nd, and 4th Fighter Groups were among the leading P-51 outfits in the Eighth Air Force.

78th Fighter Group P-47 Thunderbolts prepare for an escort mission over Germany. As long-range drop tanks became available, the Eighth Air Force's Thunderbolts were able to extend their reach deep into Germany— so deep that before the end of the war P-47s flew escort missions all the way to Berlin and back.

11

RELENTLESS PURSUIT: BIG WEEK

★ ★ ★ ★ ★

"Our little band grows smaller and smaller. Every man can work it out for himself on the fingers of one hand when his own turn is due to come."
—Heinz Knocke, Luftwaffe fighter pilot

THE FALL'S DEBACLES FINISHED OFF IRA EAKER. At the end of 1943, Arnold recast the command structure in Europe. Eaker went to the Mediterranean and never received his third star. In his place, Jimmy Doolittle took over the Eighth Air Force. Spaatz became the overall commander of U.S. Strategic Forces Europe, which included both the Eighth and the freshly established Fifteenth Air Force in Italy. The Eighth would be the left hook; the Fifteenth would be the uppercut. Together, Spaatz could use both to batter the Third Reich into submission.

In England, changes were afoot. Doolittle inspected his new command and raced around East Anglia meeting the bomber and fighter crews. Toward the end of January 1944, during a familiarization trip over to VIII Fighter Command Headquarters, he walked into Gen. William Kepner's office and saw the sign hanging on the wall. Doolittle read it over, "The first duty of the Eighth Air Force fighters is to bring the bombers back alive."

Doolittle didn't like it. He asked Kepner the source of the sign. Kepner told him that it had been something Gen. Frank Hunter had put up in the office in 1942.

"Take it down," Doolittle ordered. He told Kepner to post another one in its place that read, "The first duty of the Eighth Air Force fighters is to destroy German fighters."

When the Fifteenth Air Force was activated at the end of 1943, Spaatz took overall command of the strategic air war in Europe. He drove Doolittle relentlessly to prosecute the campaign at all costs.

When Doolittle became the Eighth Air Force's commanding officer, he embarked on a whirlwind tour to meet his men and his units. Here, he gets a short brief on the M2 .50-caliber machine gun during one of his stops in East Anglia.

Kepner loved this. It signaled a new approach to the use of his pilots. In the ensuing weeks, Doolittle made it clear he wanted Kepner's fighter jocks to channel their inner aggressiveness. In the air, their restrictions were removed. No longer would the fighters be chained to the bomber stream, unable to pursue fleeing German aircraft below 18,000 feet. Indeed, Doolittle made it clear that if the Luftwaffe's fighters were not pursued relentlessly, VIII Fighter Command was not doing its job.

At the same time, Arnold and Spaatz took a hard look at the failure of Pointblank with an eye on the upcoming invasion of France, scheduled for the late spring of 1944. In a sense, it was the Battle of Britain in reverse. Without air superiority over the battlefield, D-Day

General Jimmy Doolittle took command of the Eighth Air Force after running Twelfth Air Force in the Mediterranean Theater.

would be a disaster. A sense of urgency pushed both men forward. The Luftwaffe had to be destroyed, and they had five months to do it. Arnold told Spaatz to get it done in the air, on the ground, or by knocking out the factories that produced the Luftwaffe's interceptors.

With the arrival of the Mustang and the new long-range drop tanks, the escort fighters held the keys to victory. American intelligence consistently underestimated Germany's aircraft production, sometimes by as much as a factor of four. Even so, it became obvious to Spaatz and his staff that no matter how many bombers landed on Luftwaffe factories, its front line units would not be hurting for replacement interceptors anytime soon. Doolittle noted this as well, stressing that fuel and aviators were the Luftwaffe's major limiting factors. And in early 1944, the American strategic forces went to war against Germany's fighter pilots.

Adolf Galland, the Luftwaffe's General of the Fighters, had patched together a formidable interceptor force in the fall of 1943 by stripping other commands to keep his fighters in the air. He grabbed pilots out of army co-operation squadrons, weather recon

William Kepner replaced General Hunter as head of VIII Fighter Command. When Doolittle took over the Mighty Eighth, he went to Kepner and ordered him to go after the Luftwaffe with his fighters. It represented a major shift in strategy, one that played a key role in defeating the German Air Force in the months before D-Day.

units, and bomber geschwaders and straight from training schools to keep warm bodies in his cockpits. It had been a near run thing that fall, but thanks to the awesome bomber-killing po⋯   ⋯Messerschmitt Bf-110, Ju-88G and Me-410 Hornet, the Luftwaffe retained control of the skies over the Reich.

The equation changed in early 1944. First, Galland's heavy twin-engine fighters proved virtually helpless against aggressive P-47, P-38, and P-51 pilots. They served a useful purpose only as long as they did not have to contend with American escorts. Now, the heavies had no safe place to operate. The Fifteenth's and Eighth's fighters could roam to the far corners of the Reich, negating one of the biggest bomber-killing weapons the Luftwaffe would have in the air war.

56th Fighter Group armorers load .50-caliber ammunition into Francis "Gabby" Gabreski's P-47 Thunderbolt. The Jug carried eight machine guns, a devastating amount of firepower that could savage German fighters and ground targets alike.

Goering conversing with Adolf Galland (right) and ace Walter Nowotny on the status of the Luftwaffe's fighter force. By 1944, the Luftwaffe's jagdgeschwaders had been stretched to their breaking point by combat casualties and aircraft losses. Continuing the brutal war of attrition over the Reich required cutting many corners in training to get new pilots into the cockpits. It also required stripping other branches of the Luftwaffe of some of their pilots, diminishing the German Air Force's capabilities as a result.

Second, Galland's pilots had been given a virtual free pass in 1943. With VIII Fighter Command chained to the bombers, the German fighters could dictate the flow of air combat over the Reich. They'd launch their attacks and run for home, confident that the Americans would not pursue them. That changed on January 24, 1944, during an Eighth Air Force mission to Frankfurt. The escort fighters roamed the flanks of the bomber stream, searching for targets. In a running battle that spread all over Germany, the Americans knocked down twenty-three interceptors and lost nine fighters and only two bombers.

The Eighth needed more days like this. To secure air superiority over Western Europe before D-Day, the Luftwaffe had to be drawn out and destroyed in battle. Spaatz and his staff studied the target lists with a new eye: what would make Galland's men come up and fight?

Defeating the heavy fighter menace during deep penetration raids played a key role in cutting down bomber losses. With Mustangs and Thunderbolts able to roam deep into the Third Reich, the Bf-110s, Me-410s, and Ju-88s could not survive in the sky without the Luftwaffe providing an escort force of Fw-190s. It was a unique situation having to divert interceptors to protect other interceptors, and it degraded the Luftwaffe's ability to knock planes down.

The American fighters became so aggressive that they followed their prey down to the deck and sometimes to the ground. Here, an VIII Fighter Command pilot strafes a Bf-110 he's brought down, sending a German crewman diving for cover. Such aggressiveness ensured the Luftwaffe's defeat over its own country.

From its rocky start as a marginally effective, short-ranged fighter, the Republic P-47 developed into the VIII Fighter Command's workhorse. The Thunderbolt scored more kills and served longer in combat than the Mustang in the ETO, and thanks to long-range tanks and better pilot training in fuel management, it could operate over most of Germany by war's end.

What emerged was Operation Argument, a massive, sustained bombing campaign focused on German fighter airframe construction and ball bearings. In a sense, it was simply a modified version of Pointblank. This time, any damage done to the ground targets was simply a bonus. The real target was the Luftwaffe's interceptors sent up in response to the incoming waves of aircraft. The bomber crews would be the bait. The Mustangs and Thunderbolts would be the trap. The stage had been set for history's largest attrition-based air campaign.

Argument kicked off with a massive RAF raid on the night of February 19–20, 1944. While the 730 bombers burned out vast stretches of Leipzig, the attackers paid a terrible price. German night fighters and flak teamed up to destroy 78 British aircraft, and 569 RAF airmen were lost in the epic nocturnal duel.

The next morning, the winter weather cleared enough to get the Eighth Air Force into the air. The Liberators and Forts struck at aircraft factories at Leipzig, Gotha, and Brunswick, very selectively targeting the Bf-109, Bf-110, Fw-190, and Ju-88 airframe production facilities there. The Germans could have no doubt; the Eighth was coming after the Defenders of the Reich.

The day cost Galland's units fifty-eight fighters. In return, the Americans lost twenty-one bombers and four fighters. Big Week kicked off with a tremendous success.

JIMMY DOOLITTLE

IF MAJ. GEN. Jimmy Doolittle had never commanded the Eighth Air Force, he still would have been one of the most illustrious and famous military aviators of his generation. Born in 1896, Doolittle grew up in Nome, Alaska, joining the army in 1917. He learned to fly, but never deployed to Europe before World War I ended. Instead, he served as a flight instructor and helped train America's first generation of aerial warriors.

In the 1920s and 1930s, Doolittle earned a reputation as a remarkable racing pilot. He won the Schneider Cup in 1926, then piloted a Gee Bee R-I to victory in the 1932 Thompson Trophy. He also won the cross-country Bendix race.

In 1942, he led the legendary "Doolittle Raid"—the first bombing attack on Japan. Using B-25 Mitchell bombers, Doolittle and his men daringly took off from the deck of the USS *Hornet* hundreds of miles off the Japanese coast. Following attacks on Tokyo, the

Jimmy Doolittle, one of America's most illustrious flying generals.

Doolittle Raiders continued on to China where all crash-landed.

The attack electrified the United States and made Doolittle a national hero. Later, he took command of the Twelfth Air Force in North Africa before taking command of the Mighty Eighth in January 1944 after Eaker was sent to the Mediterranean. The move put Doolittle at center stage of the USAAF's air effort in Europe, but it also put him at odds with his two superiors, Fred Anderson and Carl Spaatz. Doolittle loved airmen and aviators. He loved visiting the bomb groups, sharing time with his men. His concern for their morale, fitness, and level of exhaustion conflicted with Spaatz and Anderson's more cold-hearted approach to keep the pressure on the Luftwaffe no matter the effect it had on the USAAF airmen carrying out the missions.

Doolittle remained one of the most beloved general officers the air force ever produced. After the war, he played a significant role in the development of America's ballistic missile program. He died in Pebble Beach, California, in 1993.

Jimmy Doolittle in the years between World War I and II. He set many racing records and earned national fame by winning the Cleveland Air Races' coveted Thompson Trophy in 1932.

A Doolittle Raider B-25 bomber struggles aloft from the USS *Hornet* on April 18, 1942.

A lone B-17 picks up a friendly P-38 as an escort for a homebound journey.

The Fifteenth Air Force played a supporting role in Big Week. Still a nascent organization, these Italy-based aviators and bombers lacked the numbers and the escort strength enjoyed by the Mighty Eighth. As a result, through February, the Fifteenth's long-range missions to heavily defended targets in Austria, Southern Germany, and Eastern Europe proved quite costly. Here, a Fifteenth Air Force B-17 goes down in flames after getting hit by flak.

The following afternoon, Doolittle's men returned to the heart of Germany and destroyed numerous targets around Brunswick. Thirty-two German fighters were written off by nightfall. That night, Goering called a conference with all his Reich defense commanders. The previous two days alarmed the Reichmarshal. The Americans had inflicted severe damage to the production lines that kept his forward units fighting. He wanted to know what his commanders could do to stop it. The conference resulted in some organizational changes that streamlined the operational chain of command. It was also agreed that when launching attacks against the bombers, the Luftwaffe would need to mass its strength in order to break through the ever-thickening layers of American escort fighters. Once massed, at least one

Some of the most heavily defended targets in Germany lay within the Fifteenth Air Force's area of responsibility.

jagdgeschwader needed to be assigned to attacking the escorts. Theoretically, this would give the other units a hole through which to attack the bombers. Previous orders had stressed the need to avoid American fighters and focus all efforts on the heavies.

On February 22, the Eighth and Fifteenth Air Forces flew their first joint mission. Almost 1,400 B-17s and B-24s thundered over the Reich, escorted by nearly a thousand white-starred fighters. The Luftwaffe threw itself at the oncoming formations. Running battles raged all across the Reich. Bad weather hampered both sides, resulting in wholesale aborts, operational accidents, and sudden encounters with the enemy in the cloud-dominated skies. General LeMay, who now commanded the Eighth Air Force's 3rd Bomb Division, noted the number of catastrophic collisions among his B-17s as they struggled to form up in the thick soup and ordered a full abort. The B-24s in the 2nd Bomb Division also received the abort signal, but not before some of them had already reached the Continent. The Liberator crews looked for targets of opportunity to bomb, which led to an unfortunate incident where one very lost B-24 crew dropped its payload on England. Another B-24 formation targeted Nijmegen, Holland, with deadly accuracy, mistaking the Dutch city for a German one. The misplaced cascade of falling high explosives and incendiaries killed 850 civilians.

The 1st Bomb Division performed the best that day. Part of the B-17s from the 384th and 303rd groups reached Aschersleben and virtually destroyed the Ju-88 factory there. The extensive damage cut production in half for the next sixty days.

Over Bernberg, the 306th Group bombed another Ju-88 plant, scoring numerous hits. But as they sped for home, they ran into a swarm of Luftwaffe fighters. The interceptors raked the group's combat box and chased them two hundred miles back to the Dutch coast. By the time the last one made its run at the 306th, the beleaguered Americans had lost seven Flying Forts. The remaining twenty-three had all been shot up.

Torn in half by a direct flak hit, a B-17 spins earthward. During the titanic air battles in February 1944, such sights—and the loss of the ten men inside those aircraft—were depressingly common.

Allied Industrial Targets in Europe

Railyard	Railyard
Ball bearings plant	Ball bearings plant
Chemical plant	Chemical plant
Oil production/refining plant	Oil production/refining plant
Aviation gas plant	Aviation gas plant
Steel plant	Steel plant
Rubber plant	Rubber plant
U-Boat base/manufacturing plant	U-Boat base/manufacturing plant
Armaments plant	Armaments plant
Aircraft plant	Aircraft plant
V-Weapons plant	V-Weapons plant

0   100   200   300 miles

NORWAY
Bergen
Oslo
Stavanger
Fredrikstad
Kristiansand
Göteborg
SWE

DENMARK
Aalborg
Esbjaelg Fredericia Copenhagen
Flensberg
Kiel
Lübeck Rostock Peenemünd
Wilhelmshaven
Emden Bremerhaven Hamburg
Bremen Stettin
Wittenberge Elbe

Inverness
Ft. William
Aberdeen
Londonderry
Glasgow Edinburgh
Hamilton
Belfast
Carlisle Newcastle
Sunderland
IRELAND Irish Sea Lancaster Scarborough
Dublin Leeds York
Limerick Liverpool Sheffield Hull
Manchester
Cork Waterford
UNITED KINGDOM
Wolverhampton Leicester XXXX
Birmingham Coventry **EIGHTH**
Swansea Gloucester Cambridge
Cardiff Oxford **NETH.**
Bristol **London** **Amsterdam**
Plymouth Southend
Southampton Canterbury Rotterdam
Portsmouth Dover Osnabrück
Calais Dunkirk Bielefeld
Cherbourg Ghent Antwerp Eindhoven Dortmund
Brest Abbeville Lille Brussels Düsseldorf Cologne
St. Brieuc Le Havre Arras Liege **BELG.** Bonn
Caen Rouen Weisbaden **GERMANY**
Rennes Seine **LUX.** Mainz Frankfurt
Laval Chartres **Paris** Metz Saarbrücken Manheim
Le Mans Heidelberg Nürnberg
Nantes Tours Blois Strasbourg Karlsruhe Regensburg
Bourges Epinal Stuttgart
FRANCE Dijon Colmar Ulm Augsburg Linz
Rochefort Limoges Mulhouse Munich
Vichy Friedrichshafen Salzburg
Bordeaux Lyon Bern Zurich Innsbruck
Bayonne **SWITZ.** Bolzano Klagenfurt
Montelimar Milan Verona Ljubljana
Santiago Lugo Turin Mestre Venice Trieste
Vigo Toulouse Avignon Parma Fiume
Pôrto (Oporto) Burgos Pamplona Montpellier Genoa Bologna **SAN MARINO**
Narbonne Nice Florence Ancona
Salamanca **ANDORRA** Marseille Pisa
SPAIN Zaragoza (Saragossa) Toulon **ITALY**
Lisbon **Madrid** Tarragon **Rome**
PORTUGAL Toledo Tortosa Barcelona XXXX
Tagus **FIFTHTEEN**
Valencia Golfo de Valencia Naples
Sevilla Balearic Islands Salerno
Golfo Puerto de Cádiz Cádiz Alicante **Sardinia**
Málaga Cartagena Corsica
Tangier Gibraltar Almería
Spanish Morocco
Rabat Palermo Messina
Casablanca Oran Algiers Sicily
Fez Bougie Philippeville Bizerte
Morocco Oujda Constantine **Tunis**
(France) **Algeria** XXXX
(France) Kairouan Sousse **NINTH**
Tunisia Malta
(France) Sfax (British)

Atlantic Ocean
Bay of Biscay
North Sea
English Channel
Mediterranean Sea
Ligurian Sea
Tyrrhenian Sea
Adriatic

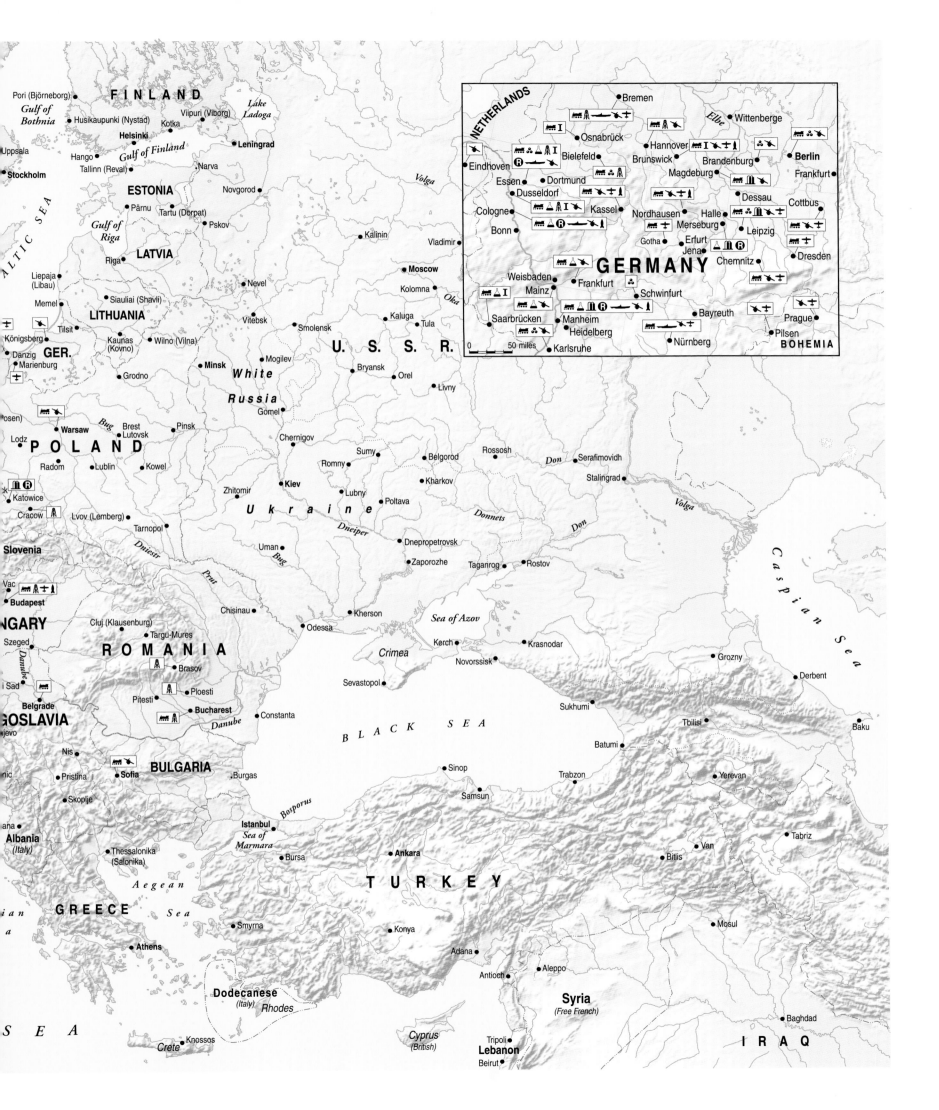

Frantic ground crewmen fight to snuff the flames out on a stricken 401st Bomb Group Flying Fort.

A 15th Air Force B-24 gunner after a mission.

The Luftwaffe wrote off another fifty-two fighters by sunset. Forty-one Forts and Liberators went down—16 percent of the Eighth Air Force's bombers—along with eleven VIII Fighter Command aircraft. The Fifteenth Air Force suffered 10 percent losses. It had been a brutal day for the USAAF.

Doolittle wanted to give his bomber crews a break. He reported to Spaatz and his operations chief, Maj. Gen. Fred Anderson, that his overtaxed airmen were subsisting on a diet of "Benzedrine and sleeping pills" to keep functioning and flying. Spaatz and Anderson vetoed the break. Anderson in particular believed the Doolittle consistently lost sight of the mission as a result of his attachment to his men. The strain between the two generals would grow in the days and weeks ahead.

Weather ended up scrubbing the scheduled missions for the twenty-third, so the Mighty Eighth's airmen did get a break. But then again, so did the Luftwaffe's exhausted fighter pilots, some of whom had been flying three or four missions a day in skies crowded with American aircraft.

On February 24, the Americans returned, flying missions to Schweinfurt again and the aircraft factories in the cities of Gotha, Kreising, and Posen. The winter weather hampered operations once again. LeMay's 3rd Bomb Division was supposed to hit targets along the Baltic coast in a very daring, unescorted strike. When the Forts got to their assigned areas, layers of clouds obscured the primary targets. Instead, the bombers turned for the city of Rostock and pummeled it before heading back over the North Sea for home.

The B-17s of the 1st Bomb Division found blue skies over Schweinfurt that miraculously were devoid of marauding Messerschmitts and Focke-Wulfs. The bombardiers took advantage of the opportunity and blasted the ball bearings factories there until little more than rubble remained.

Few targets were better defended and more dangerous for the Fifteenth Air Force than Vienna. Here, a Fifteenth Air Force Liberator struggles through a sky full of flak after getting hit in the right inboard engine.

Fifteenth Air Force B-24 over Italy during a mission in 1944.

If the Forts found the day's missions easier than expected, the Liberators of the 2nd Bomb Division paid the price for their easy entry over Germany. The Luftwaffe's ground controllers vectored the bulk of the available fighters at the B-24 stream heading for Gotha. Eighty minutes from their Initial Point, the Luftwaffe pilots swarmed over the leading Liberator groups.

The 389th Bomb Group formed the tip of the divisional spear. In a freakish twist of fate, as the Liberator crews battled their way to Gotha's Bf-110 factories, the group's

A battle-damaged Thunderbolt after crash-landing back in England. When the VIII Fighter Command began hitting airfields, trains, and other ground targets, such efforts drew considerable light and medium anti-aircraft fire that took a steady toll on the attacking aircraft.

Smoke and flames rise over a target area as a B-17 combat wing reaches its release point.

lead aircraft suffered an oxygen system failure. As the B-24 veered out of formation, the bombardier passed out and accidentally toggled off his bombs. The rest of the group followed suit and missed the factories completely. Moments later, the interceptors waded into the group and flamed six of the silver-winged Libs.

Behind the 389th came the 445th Bomb Group. They stayed as tight as a Liberator outfit could, the gunners tracking incoming fighters and snapping out short bursts at them. The Germans proved relentless, using everything from cannon and rocket fire to aerial cables and air-burst bombs to try to bring the Liberators down. One by one, the group's B-24s caught fire and fell out of formation. Others limped along, streaming thick tongues of black smoke behind savaged engines. By the time the survivors limped home to England, thirteen of the 445th's twenty-five Liberators were little more than smoking craters on the Continent. Of the remaining twelve, nine had been heavily damaged.

The 392nd, another B-24 group, somehow managed the best bomb run of the day despite repeated fighter attacks. The group's bombardier put 98 percent of the unit's ordnance within two thousand feet of the Bf-110 factories at Gotha. It was one of the best operational examples of precision bombing of the war, but the 392nd did not get away unscathed. Seven of its B-24s went down in flames.

To the south, the Fifteenth Air Force struck an aircraft plant at Steyr, Austria. The long-range mission from Italy cost the Fifteenth 20 percent of the bombers dispatched. Altogether, Spaatz's two air forces lost over seventy bombers. The Luftwaffe wrote off about sixty of its interceptors.

Doolittle looked around East Anglia and saw nothing but burnt-out airmen, bullet scarred bombers, and ground crewmen working round the clock to patch planes together for the next mission. Once again, he begged Anderson and Spaatz to give his men a break.

A formation of Fifteenth Air Force B-17 Flying Fortresses over Eastern Europe in 1944. This photo achieved a measure of fame when it appeared in the movie *The Best Years of Our Lives*. In one scene, Dana Andrews's character, Fred Derry, shows his war bride this photo, and she was so clueless to what he experienced she asked what the little black clouds were.

Anderson told him to shut up and do his job. The targets for February 25 included Regensburg, the huge Messerschmitt 109 plant at Augsburg, plus the ball bearings factory in Stuttgart. It would be another maximum effort, a two-air-force strike.

The Fifteen Air Force drew the Regensburg mission. About 140 of its bombers reached the target, only to be assailed by flak and fighters. Thirty-nine of its Forts and Libs went down—a brutal 20 percent of the attacking force.

The Eighth followed up the Fifteenth with a hundred-Fort raid on Regensburg later that day. This move caught the Reich's defenders by surprise and the Americans found the skies far less hostile than they were earlier in the day. The heavies utterly destroyed the Bf-109 factory there in another remarkable display of accuracy.

Altogether, the day cost the USAAF another seventy four-engined bombers. The Luftwaffe suffered just as hard, and had started to run out of fresh bodies to fill the cockpits of the available interceptors. In fact, the commander of the I Fighter Corps subsequently wrote, "In the long run, our forces are fighting a hopeless battle." When February finally drew to a close, the Luftwaffe's fighter force had lost a total of 434 pilots, almost 18 percent of its total strength. The daylight battle over the Reich was bleeding the jagdgeschwaders white.

Big Week ended after the missions on the twenty-fifth. The Fifteen and Eighth Air Forces had flown a combined 3,823 bomber sorties while the RAF put 2,351 over Germany at night. Together, the Allies dropped 18,291 tons of bombs on eighteen aircraft factories and two ball bearings plants. The week cost the Luftwaffe at least a hundred pilots and almost

The air war mingled physical discomfort and boredom with searing moments of sudden violence. Here, an 88mm flak hit has ripped a Fifteenth Air Force B-24 in half.

three hundred interceptors. The USAAF lost 227 bombers; the RAF lost another 157. Some five thousand RAF and USAAF airmen died, returned to England or Italy wounded, or simply went missing over the flak-filled German skies.

Big Week inflicted significant damage on the targeted German factories. The Regensburg Bf-109 plant was totally destroyed, which effectively denied the Luftwaffe about 750 fighters. At Augsburg, 160 freshly completed aircraft were either destroyed or damaged in the bombing, and further production did not resume for over two weeks.

The factories weren't the real targets though; the Luftwaffe was. And in meeting the American maximum effort with one of their own, the defenders of the Reich had been stretched beyond their endurance. The Americans finally had the Luftwaffe on the ropes. Now, they needed to deliver the knock-out blow.

They didn't make it quite home. The end of a battle-damaged B-24 and its crew of ten dedicated young Americans.

A 91st Bomb Group Flying Fort over the Messerschmitt plant at Augsburg, Germany, during Big Week on February 25, 1944.

Robert S. Johnson, one of the leading 56th Fighter Group aces, is credited today with twenty-seven aerial victories. He shot down eight German fighters in one month during the intense air battles over Germany in the spring of 1944. For a time, he was the Eighth Air Force's leading fighter ace.

12

TIPPING POINT

★ ★ ★ ★ ★

"The strained manpower situation in units operating in defense of the Reich demands urgently the further bringing up of experienced flying personnel from other arms of the service . . . for the maintenance of the fighter arm."
—*Adolf Galland, General of the Fighters, March 1944*

SINCE NOVEMBER 1943, the RAF had waged a singular campaign against the German capital. In what became known as the "The Battle of Berlin," the British launched sixteen maximum effort raids on the city through the winter of 1943–1944. Bomber Harris declared, "It may cost us a thousand bombers, but it will cost Germany the war."

By this point in the war, Bomber Command had come up the night attack learning curve. Using early electronic countermeasures techniques, such as "window" or chaff to spoof German radars, the British had on occasion been able to throw the Luftwaffe off its game and hit targets without significant interception. New navigation aids helped considerably, and the number of aircraft that actually bombed the primary target steadily increased through 1943 and 1944. Radar became a staple for both the heavy bombers and the night fighters sent out to protect them. And by mid-1943, a radio transponder system known as "Oboe" provided decent poor weather guidance to a target area. Oboe used two stations back in England that homed in on a radio beacon carried by a pathfinder DeHaviland Mosquito. The stations would pinpoint the pathfinder's location and guide it to the target area. Once in the right place, the Mossies would release parachute flares to mark the area. Further pathfinders would then drop incendiary bombs

The versatile DeHaviland Mosquito played a significant role in Bomber Command's operations in 1943 and 1944. Some flew nocturnal hunting missions as night fighters, prowling the flanks of the bomber stream to pick off German Bf-110s and Me-410s. Other Mossies flew ahead of the Lancasters and Halifaxes to mark the target area in the pathfinder role.

The Battle of Berlin began in November 1943 at a time when Bomber Command had finally made the jump from a twin-engine dominated force to one far more capable, thanks to the massive influx of Halifaxes and Lancasters. Nevertheless, Berlin was the most heavily defended target in the world at that time, and Bomber Command lost five hundred aircraft trying to break the German people's morale with the destruction sown on their city.

on the flares, creating a conflagration in the target area that served as the aim point for the rest of the bomber stream. With Oboe, the heavies could sometimes strike their targets with nearly the same level of accuracy that the Norden bombsight possessed. It was used extensively in the Ruhr Valley, but it could not operate all the way to Berlin due to the curvature of the earth. For such missions, Bomber Command relied on the H2S radar system carried by its Lancasters and Halifaxes.

By late 1943, the Wellington was being phased out of front line service as more Halifaxes and Lancasters rolled off the production line. The enormous amount of material, treasure, and humanity Great Britain poured into Bomber Command finally began to pay dividends. By the time the Battle of Berlin began, the vast majority of the squadrons committed to it flew Lancasters. Eventually, Lanc crews carried out just over seven thousand sorties over the Nazi capital out of about nine thousand total during the campaign.

The first night's attacks resulted in only nine bombers lost. Encouraged, Bomber Command struck again a few nights later. Between missions to Berlin, the RAF continued hitting cities in the Ruhr and elsewhere throughout Germany. The low loss rate did not hold. As the campaign wore on, Luftwaffe night fighters—including now the deadly effective Heinkel 219 "Owl"—found their way into bomber stream and took a devastating toll. From November 18 until the end of March, the campaign cost the RAF over a thousand aircraft (five hundred alone on the Berlin raids).

The grinding loss rate appalled the crews, who felt as if they were being thrown away for little purpose. Morale plummeted. One squadron alone suffered over 100 percent losses in three months. On some missions, the RAF senior leadership questioned the resolve of the crews in pressing home their attacks on Berlin. After the campaign, one group commander, Air Vice Marshal Bennett, summed up the situation: "There can be no doubt that a very large number of crews failed to carry out their attacks during the Battle of Berlin in their customary determined manner."

While losing over 1,000 bombers and another 1,600 damaged (plus 3,700 aircrew), Bomber Command inflicted extensive damage on Berlin. By the end of the campaign in March

The Battle of Berlin profoundly affected the surviving Bomber Command aircrews. Morale plummeted, especially after it appeared all the sacrifices the men had made seemed all for nothing. Much of Berlin lay in ruins, but the German people seemed ever more resolved to fighting on. From the end of the Battle of Berlin to May 1945, the RAF crews tasked with carrying the offensive to the German people grew increasingly fatalistic. Having a 24 percent chance of surviving the campaign unscathed, safe at home in England were not odds anyone could endure with perpetual good cheer.

A formation of 44 Squadron Lancs high over England. The Germans learned to exploit the Lancaster's lack of a belly turret by using their "Jazz Music"-equipped Bf-110s to creep under the Avros and fire up into them while safely inside the RAF aircraft's blind spot.

Fires burn in the city streets below, silhouetting a Lancaster in its hellish glow. During some raids, the firestorms created turbulence and smoke clouds over ten thousand feet above the urban areas being consumed. RAF crews could navigate to the target by the flames, which could sometimes be seen from sixty miles away.

The Battle of Berlin and all its associated raids cost Bomber Command a thousand aircraft from November 1943 to March 1944. Here, a Halifax goes down after losing its right vertical stabilizer.

Bomber Command ground crews put the final touches on a Lancaster before the night's mission. The dedication and work ethic the ground crews gave to their squadrons made the sustained air war against Germany possible. Without their devotion, the out-of-commission rates would have crippled the bombing effort. Yet, their thankless jobs received little recognition during the war or after.

The end of a very long day for an Eighth Air Force B-17 crew. The furious pace Spaatz and Anderson set for the crews in the spring of 1944 alarmed Doolittle, who fought whenever he could to give his men some time off.

1944, almost half a million Germans had been left homeless by the British raids. Another fourteen thousand had been killed or injured.

Yet, German morale did not crumble. Instead the people Harris sought to kill or coerce into surrender only grew more resolute to continue the fight. Despite the damage to Berlin's factories, war production quickly increased in 1944. Despite the hardships inflicted by the nocturnal bombers, the Germans would not quit. Four years after the London Blitz failed, the Battle of Berlin proved Douhet wrong again.

Bomber Command suffered a clear defeat over Berlin that winter. The crews started to wonder what the point of all this sacrifice was when nothing tangible ever seemed to be gained by it. Some historians have compared the crisis within Bomber Command in the spring of 1944 to the one the British Army experienced in France in 1917. Morale never collapsed, but it never fully recovered. A fatalistic resolve permeated Bomber Command until the end of the war.

Meanwhile, Doolittle's Eighth Air Force crews finished out February with a 20 percent overall loss rate among the bombers. Five percent was considered sustainable in both the RAF and the USAAF. Doolittle continued to want to give his airmen time to recover, but his bosses, Fred Anderson and Spaatz, demanded that he maintain the pressure on the Luftwaffe.

To do so, the USAAF had to find another target that would force the Germans to come out and fight. Just as the British lost the Battle of Berlin, Spaatz stepped in and ordered the Mighty Eighth to hit the German capital in broad daylight. For the first time, the Americans would not target a specific factory complex. Instead, Berlin was to be carpet bombed under the winter sun. In retrospect, that shift away from precision targeting to area targeting marked a major step forward in the evolution of American aerial strategy, one that lead ultimately to the firebombing of Tokyo and the atomic attacks on Nagasaki and Hiroshima.

The RAF's Mosquito ranked as the best all-purpose aircraft of World War II. It served as a night fighter, a strike aircraft, a fighter-bomber, as well as a pathfinder and reconnaissance platform. Here, a Mosquito lays waste to German ships caught at anchor in a Norwegian fjord in the summer of 1944.

Pilots of the Eighth Air Force's legendary 4th Fighter Group pose for a snapshot prior to a mission in 1944.

Berlin lay 1,100 miles from the bomber bases in East Anglia. The distance involved had already cost the British dearly. During the night raids, the Luftwaffe took to intercepting the RAF over the North Sea, continuing the interceptions all the way to Berlin, then pursuing them almost to the British coast on their way out. With such a long exposure period, the RAF lost scores of bombers on these missions.

In the first week of March, the Eighth went to Berlin. Weather was an obstacle from the outset. The final days of winter left the Continent blanketed in thick cloud cover. It didn't matter. Spaatz ordered the bombers into the air anyway.

For the survivors of the Big Week, the sight of red ribbon stretching all the way to Berlin on the briefing room's wall map had a profound affect two weeks later. Groans, whistles, dead silence greeted the news of the target.

It didn't help that the weather was awful. The first raid, set for March 3, misfired due to heavy clouds and storms the bombers encountered. Only the B-24s of the 3rd Bomb Division reached Berlin. The American campaign against the capital started more with a whimper than a bang.

The next day, snow fell in East Anglia. Doolittle wanted to scrub the mission. Anderson and Spaatz ordered him to get the bombers in the air. Five hundred Forts and Liberators headed for the target, only to run into even more appalling weather. Only sixty-nine tons of ordnance landed on Berlin.

In the furious air battles of Big Week and Berlin, the 4th Fighter Group's tandem aces, Don Gentile and Johnny Godfrey, rose to fame as the Eighth Air Force's most famous fighting pair. Gentile scored 19.83 aerial kills and 6 more on the ground during his combat career. Godfrey received credit for 28.99 air and ground kills before he himself was shot down and taken prisoner in the late summer of 1944.

A battle-damaged Fort burns on a farmer's field back in East Anglia, having failed to reach its airfield after a mission over Germany.

That night, Doolittle wanted to give his airmen off-base passes. He saw their fatigue, saw their stress, and continued to worry that Spaatz and Anderson were pushing them beyond human endurance. They needed a break. Spaatz said no. The passes were cancelled.

The weather intervened and gave the crews the break they needed. Severe storms and fog grounded the Eighth Air Force on March 5. The next day, though, Spaatz wanted every bird in the air. Despite heavy cloud cover, Doolittle gave the "Go" order and 730 bombers found their way through the soup to wing their way east.

The Luftwaffe rose to challenge them with a vengeance. Vectored into elements of the 1st Bomb Division, an epic air battle erupted over the German frontier as waves of interceptors

56th Fighter Group ace Francis Gabreski received national press for his exploits over Germany while scoring twenty-eight air and ground kills. But even as the veteran pilots of VIII Fighter Command took a heavy toll of the Luftwaffe's aces defending the Third Reich, the merciless war of attrition claimed plenty of American ones as well. Gabreski crash-landed during a strafing run against a German airfield in July 1944 and was taken prisoner. By the end of the summer, the Luftstalags held many of the VIII's top aces, including fellow Wolfpack ace and former commanding officer Hubert "Hub" Zemke.

waded into the 91st, 92nd, and 381st Bomb Groups. Frantic gunners laid on their triggers as the 109s and 190s flashed past through their formations. The 91st took a beating, losing six Forts and sixty men. The other two groups in the wing lost seven more.

Moments later, a squadron of Messerschmitt Bf-109s slipped through the escort screen to make a head-on attack on the 457th Bomb Group. One German pilot misjudged his run and collided into 2nd Lt. Roy Graves' B-17. Locked together, the wreckage from both planes spun into Graves' wingman, 2nd Lt. Eugene Whalen's Fort.

The formations soldiered forward. Fresh interceptors struck the unluckiest group in the Eighth Air Force. This was the Bloody Hundredth, and again they earned their reputation. Caught unprotected by Mustangs or Thunderbolts, the Hundredth encountered upwards of a hundred German fighters or more. In seconds, they dove down into the American combat box in another furious head on pass. The entire 350th Bomb Squadron—the high element in the box that day—went down in flames. Ten bombers in a blink of an eye. Still the buzz saw continued. Before their return to England, the 100th Bomb Group lost fifteen of its twenty planes.

The Eighth made no effort to hide their destination. The Luftwaffe controllers scrambled everything that could fly and fight. Even units that were serving on the Eastern Front received orders taking them over Berlin. The fighting raged across the length of the Reich until late afternoon when the final battle-damaged burning bombers crash-landed back in East Anglia.

Spaatz was right: The Germans would fight for Berlin. Sixty-nine bombers had gone down during the day. The Germans lost sixty-six fighters.

Francis Gabreski and members of the 56th Fighter Group stage a celebratory shot in the group's officer's club at Halesworth.

Forts of the 384th Bomb Group over Berlin during the March 6, 1944, raid. The lead bomber, *Shack Rabbit*, survived the air war only another month. During an April 24, 1944, raid to Oberpfaffenhofen, *Shack Rabbit* was shot down over France. The Fort's pilot, Lt. Walter L. Harvey, and four other members of the crew were able to escape back to England, thanks to the French underground. The 384th Bomb Group lost eight bombers that day, over a quarter of its strength.

The next day the weather closed in, but on March 8, Spaatz ordered the Eighth to hit Berlin again. Thirty-seven bombers went down. The Luftwaffe lost fifty-five interceptors.

Worn out, pushed to the edge of human endurance, the German pilots had reached a breaking point. Since the Americans commenced attacks on Berlin, some of the Luftwaffe's best fighter leaders had been killed in the Reich's cloud-strewn skies. Egon Mayer, Anton Hackl, Hugo Frey, Gerhard Loos, and Rudolf Ehrenberger—all bomber-killing experts and aces with a combined 471 aerial victories—had died in battle between March 2–8.

The Luftwaffe simply couldn't sustain the loss of such veteran pilots. By this point in the war, their experience and leadership were the only things holding together the fighter geschwaders.

On the other side of the fence, the American crews had been pushed to the ragged edge of exhaustion as well. Doolittle fretted and worried about them, but Spaatz and Anderson were unrelenting. They laid on another strike against Berlin for March 9. There would be no respite for the crews, many of whom had already flown on every other mission to the capital.

As an engine mechanic goes about his business, an armorer pauses as a local farmer's wife feeds her ducks right there in the parking area of the Eighth Air Force station. Civilians lived clustered around the edges of the American bases and frequently came and went as they saw fit.

One of the 2nd Bomb Division's B-24 groups makes its way toward Berlin during the March 6, 1944, raid.

The 306th Bomb Group, 1st Division, closing in on Berlin during the Mighty Eighth's epic campaign against the German capital. The Americans succeeded in delivering a body blow to the Luftwaffe by making its fighter force come out and fight to defend Berlin.

A 56th Fighter Group Wolfpack P-47D Razorback Thunderbolt escorting a B-17 formation during one of the March Berlin raids. This particular P-47 survived the brutal attrition over Europe until August 3, 1944, when it was shot down over Europe.

That morning, the crews gathered in the briefing room and learned they would bomb Berlin again. Given the desperate battles and loss of so many friends over the past week, it would be difficult to underestimate the fear and despair that the news of the day's target evoked in these young Americans. Some of those men were short-timers; this would be their twenty-fifth mission. Instead of an easy milk run and a flight back home, they faced another grueling ordeal over the heart of the Reich. One such veteran described how he became a "nervous wreck" as he and his comrades struggled to finish their last four missions in the midst of this blitz on Berlin.

The 94th Bomb Group over Berlin in early March. The pace of combat operations and the level of attrition during the spring of 1944 made chances of survival quite dicey for the crews of these B-17s. The Fort in the picture's foreground was severely damaged a few weeks later during a raid on Brunswick on March 23, 1944. The crew managed to coax the crippled bird to the English Channel, but they finally had to set it down in the water. All aboard were killed.

Throughout the Berlin campaign, the weather played havoc with the Eighth's operations. Several days' raids had to be canceled, especially after an unseasonal snowstorm dusted the East Anglia bomber stations.

Chow Hound, a 91st Bomb Group B-17 over Berlin during the March 8, 1944, mission. Thirty-seven bombers went down during this raid on the Reich's capital, but the previous week's fighting had hammered the Luftwaffe's interceptor force. The next day, the Germans could not defend Berlin against one more attack, and the Eighth suffered only light losses. Chow Hound and her crew survived the offensive against Berlin, only to be lost over France in August. Nine men went down with their B-17 and died.

A 93rd Bomb Group B-24 en route to Friedrichshafen. After the Berlin campaign, the Eighth Air Force did not relent. Near daily deep penetration raids sustained the pressure through March and April, forcing the Luftwaffe's exhausted interceptor pilots to rise and do battle against ever-longer odds. This particular B-24 endured the spring offensive before D-Day, only to go down over Belgium on September 21, 1944.

A 34th Bomb Group B-24 on its bomb run. The Eighth Air Force expanded to include by the Berlin raids two bomb divisions of B-17s and one of B-24s.

Heavy cloud cover obscured most of Germany that day. The bombers hit Berlin and other cities using radar to guide them into the target areas. But instead of swarms of German fighters to greet them, the grey winter skies were devoid of interceptors. Weather, catastrophic losses, and fatigue conspired to keep the Luftwaffe on the ground. Flak shot down nine bombers. Berlin had been raided, and the Germans could no longer defend it. A turning point had been reached. By the end of the month, the Luftwaffe lost 56 percent of its available fighters and 22 percent of its interceptor pilots. Twenty-five more veteran aces would die attacking the bomber streams between March and May.

The commander of the fighter defenses in the north (Jagdgruppe I), later remarked, "The American forces captured air supremacy over almost the entire Reich . . . and this meant the complete collapse of Germay's position as an air power."

Major Jim Howard, a former Flying Tiger ace with six kills, joined the 354th Fighter Group as a squadron commander in time to reach England with the unit in December 1943. On January 11, 1944, he encountered about thirty Luftwaffe fighters attacking the B-17s of the 401st Bomb Group. Alone, Howard waded into the German interceptors and shot down six of them. He saved the 401st from suffering the fate of so many other bomber groups that had been singled out by the Luftwaffe's fighters. For his actions that day, Howard received the Medal of Honor, the only fighter pilot in the Eighth Air Force to be so decorated.

Jim Howard, George Bickell, and Owen Seaman, the 354th Fighter Group's squadron commanders in early 1944, pose on the flight line before a mission. Bickell and Seaman had both been at Pearl Harbor on December 7, 1941, and had endured the Japanese surprise attack. Without the 354th and the arrival of more P-51 Mustangs in theater, the Berlin strikes in March would never have been possible.

It would not be easy. Plenty of fight remained in the jagdgeschwaders, and at times they could inflict serious damage. On March 18, they punished the 2nd Bomb Division's B-24s for a terrible mistake made over Friedrichshafen when the 44th Group executed a 360-degree circle over the target area. The trailing groups, confused by the unscheduled move, abandoned their bomb runs and switched to a secondary target. In the process, the Liberators became strung out. At that moment, the Luftwaffe hit them with seventy-five fighters. Attacking in waves of six, they sent fifteen 392nd Group B-24s down in flames.

Old Glory was one of them. Damaged by flak that had already wounded or killed two members of the crew, the Liberator struggled to maintain formation with one engine feathered and two fires raging. As the pilots fought to save the aircraft, German fighters

continued on page 231

Starting a 381st Bomb Group B-17's engines required coordination between pilots and ground crews. Here, a ground crewman checks out the right inboard engine as it sputters to life, keeping a fire extinguisher handy in case something went wrong.

The 452nd Bomb Group over Berlin during the March 9, 1944, raid. The surprised Americans, jaded and cautious from the bloodbaths over Berlin since March 2, expected heavy losses. Instead, they found the cloudy skies virtually free of Luftwaffe interceptors.

Hub Zemke ranks as one of the greatest fighter leaders of World War II. He shaped the 56th Fighter Group into one of the most effective in the history of the USAAF. He scored 17.75 confirmed kills during his tenure in the VIII Fighter Command before being lost over Germany in October 1944. He spent the rest of the war in a POW camp.

During the spring and summer of 1944, the skies over Germany filled with contrails almost every day.

Little Miss Mischief after a mission over Nazi-held Europe. Thanks to the tireless efforts of the ground crews, such crash-landings rarely kept a B-17 out of action long. They performed miracles with mechanical ingenuity.

A crippled Fort from the 381st Bomb Group belly-lands back in England. The weight of the aircraft usually crushed the ball turret during such desperate landings. If the turret had jammed or had been put out of action by battle damage, the gunner inside faced a grim reality: his life for the rest of the crew's.

A German-eye view of a 452nd Bomb Group B-17G about to drop its bombs on Berlin during a raid in the spring of 1944.

The gut-check moment: on the bomb run, straight and level, sitting targets . . . the crews could only pray they would come through unscathed. It all came down to chance—and perhaps faith.

Hauptmann Anton Hackl, one of the Luftwaffe's leading bomber-killers, was among the twenty-eight German aces to be killed during the furious fighting in the spring of 1944. The attrition rate on German pilots grew so severe that their life expectancy in combat averaged eight to thirty days.

Another Luftwaffe casualty during the spring was 275-kill ace Gunther Rall. He was wounded in action flying against the Americans and was knocked out of action for several weeks.

Another shot of the 452nd Bomb Group at its release point over Berlin, March 6, 1944.

pounced. Bullets flayed the fuselage. The nose gunner cried out for help. The next attack knocked out the oxygen system; the Lib started to buck and heave, growing increasingly out of control. The tail gunner had moved forward and was in the waist when an oxygen bottle overhead took a direct hit and exploded. The blast threw the tail gunner, Chester Strickler, straight through the waist window. As he parachuted to the ground, the Liberator was reduced to falling debris. He was its lone survivor.

Though the tipping point had been reached, plenty of desperate, hard fighting remained.

The remains of a battle-damaged B-24 after crashing back in England. Six wounded, four miraculously escaped harm.

A graphic display of the P-51's ruggedness at the 364th Fighter Group's home station in East Anglia.

13

DESTRUCTION AND DISTRACTION

"I would rather have a mass of aircraft standing around unable to fly owing to a lack of petrol than not have any at all."
—*Herman Goering*

LIKE WINGED PARTISANS, THE VIII FIGHTER COMMAND STRUCK. Mustangs and Thunderbolts, cut loose from bomber apron strings, roamed low across Nazi-held Europe in search of anything worth blowing up. Trucks, staff cars, ammunition dumps, airfields, flak batteries, and trains became choice targets. Trains served as bullet magnet. If they moved in daylight anywhere in Western Europe that spring of 1944, chances were good an Allied fighter would drop down out of the clouds and rake it with gunfire. The pilots especially loved to blow up the locomotives. Fifty-caliber rounds could do a lot of damage very quickly, and a stricken locomotive would erupt in clouds of white steam when hit.

Ace Max Lamb, an original member of the 354th "Pioneer Mustangs," found a train running along an open stretch of flat farmland. He led a flight of four P-51s down to flay the locomotive with machine gun fire. When it exploded, hundreds of Wehrmacht soldiers poured out of the now-stationary passenger cars. Line abreast, almost wing-to-wing, the four Mustangs made pass after pass at the soldiers, their sixteen M2 fifties slaughtering dozens in with every run. Caught without any cover, the soldiers panicked and either ran for it or lay flat and prayed. By the time the last spent casing fell from Lamb's wing, the better part of a battalion had been mauled by four American pilots.

Welcome to the new air war, where fighter-bombers ruled the wild blue and nothing below was safe. With two months left to go before D-Day, Doolittle unleashed Kepner's fighters and told

Max Lamb's North American ride. Gentle and soft-spoken, Lamb was a capable and dedicated pilot who finished the war with 7.5 confirmed kills.

Once the VIII Fighter Command was unleashed from rigid bomber escort tactics, the Luftwaffe had no safe place.

Strafing trains became serious sport for the pilots of VIII Fighter Command. Destroying locomotives and rolling stock helped cripple the Wehrmacht's strategic mobility and made it very difficult for the Germans to push reinforcements into Normandy.

The RAF's Spitfires from the 2nd Tactical Air Force joined in the strafing and ground attack campaign throughout northwest Europe. During the Normandy campaign, a Spitfire caught Field Marshall Erwin Rommel's staff car on a narrow French lane, strafed it, and wounded the legendary German panzer leader.

them to wreak havoc on anything worth a bullet. At first, this applied only to VIII Fighter Command units that had completed their escort duties for the day. En route home from England, the pilots were told to fly low and go hunting. Starting in April this tactic evolved into specific missions. Using Ultra and other intelligence sources, the Eighth pinpointed the location of many Luftwaffe units based in France and Germany. On April 5, the VIII Fighter Command targeted some of those airfields. Bad weather hampered the operation, but two groups found their way to their targets and destroyed ninety-eight aircraft on the ground or in the air.

None of this would have been possible if the Luftwaffe still owned the airspace over the Continent. Big Week and Berlin set the conditions for this new offensive. And in concert with the fighter-bomber attacks, the RAF's heavies, the Allied tactical air forces and Spaatz's command worked on the pre-invasion "Transportation Plan." Harris thought it was a useless

A Polish-flown Spitfire airborne over England. The Poles never lost their extreme aggressiveness and took to the strafing campaign with singular fury.

A 78th Fighter Group P-47D razorback Thunderbolt. Though designed as a high-altitude fighter, the Jug's incredible ruggedness, ordnance capacity, and tremendous firepower transformed it into the best fighter-bomber of World War II.

Don Gentile's famous *Shangri-La*, one of the best-known Mustangs of the European air war. He would run afoul of his commanding officer, Don Blakeslee, for flat-hatting (flying very low to the ground) in this aircraft for some reporters in spring 1944.

While stunting for his crowd of media types, Gentile crashed his Mustang and wrecked it. Blakeslee was so furious that he grounded Gentile and sent him home, ending his combat career.

diversion and wanted to keep his men focused on turning German cities into rubble. But the battlefield preparation for D-Day was truly massive in scope and required every aircraft to carry out.

The Transportation Plan called for sealing off the Normandy area from the rest of Europe by destroying the rail and road network in Western Europe. By knocking out bridges, destroying railroad yards, carpet bombing road intersections, and strafing trains and vehicles, the Allies hoped to prevent the Germans from quickly reinforcing their units in Normandy. Since the Wehrmacht had a larger force available than what the Allies could land and sustain on the Continent, the only way the invasion could succeed was if the Germans could not get more men and supplies to the new front.

Through April the Allied strategic forces split their effort between long-range strikes into Germany and supporting the transportation plan.

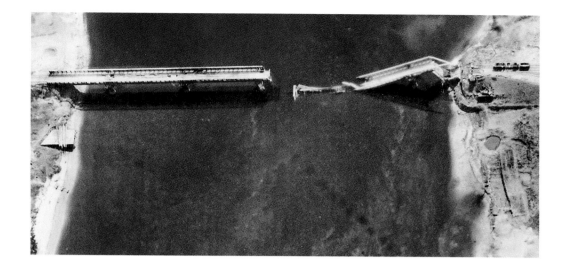

Part of the air plan in support of the Normandy operation called for the destruction of France's road and rail infrastructure leading to the future battlefield. Here, a bridge over the Seine River has been dropped by a well-executed strike.

With drop tanks, all things were possible. With enough gas to fly almost anywhere in the Third Reich, the Luftwaffe lost its ability to find sanctuary from the Mighty Eighth's roaming fighters. Even training units were caught and thrashed by the Mustangs, Thunderbolts, and Lightnings.

Preparing for another long-range mission over Germany.

Meanwhile, the Eighth Air Force's Mustangs, Lightnings, and Thunderbolts continued their depredations all the way into southern Germany.

By month's end, the Germans knocked down 409 Eighth Air Force bombers, more than any other month. In the fall of 1943, such losses would have crippled the American campaign. But two seasons later, the USAAF's build-up and replacement rate was so robust that the Eighth continued to grow even as it lost four thousand men in a four week span.

Though the Luftwaffe scored high in April, it was a Pyrrhic victory. The month's dogfights killed or wounded 489 pilots. The defenders of the Reich proper suffered a 38-percent attrition rate. What's more, the Luftwaffe's training command only graduated 376

To avoid friendly fire incidents, the Allies painted their aircraft with white and black "invasion" stripes in the days before the Normandy landings. This was supposed to give the warships in the Channel and the ground troops on the beachhead a quick way to recognize Allied aircraft.

The Jug's legendary ruggedness saved many pilots from death or captivity. Here, a 350th Fighter Group P-47 pilot brought his bird home after taking a hit in the oil system. Barely able to see through the viscous fluid sprayed all over his canopy, he nevertheless managed to get down safely.

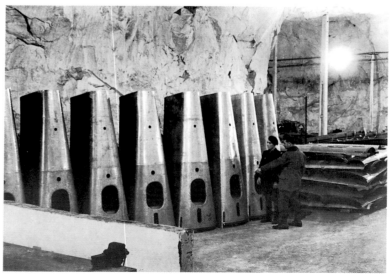

As the strategic bombing campaign demolished Germany's aviation factories, the Third Reich began dispersing the industry into vast underground mines and facilities. Buried deep beneath the surface, these plants could not be destroyed by Allied bombs.

cadets that month. Most of these aviators possessed only half the flight hours of their grass-green Allied enemies. As the intensity of the air campaign escalated, such neophytes thrown in half-prepared were little more than airborne cannon fodder.

Meanwhile, with a shortfall of almost a hundred warm bodies for his cockpits, Galland had to ask for more crews from the bomber and reconnaissance arms, thus weakening on the eve of D-Day the offensive striking power the Germans possessed.

In May, General Eisenhower released the strategic bombers from their pre-Normandy prep work. Spaatz took the opportunity to open a new offensive against Germany. This time, instead of going after Berlin or the aircraft industry, he selected the Reich's oil producing

To build its newest-generation aircraft, the Nazis used slave laborers—Jews or Russians or Slavs rounded up to work under appalling conditions until they died.

A German Gr. 21 rocket scores a near miss on a B-17. The Gr. 21s were most effective at dispersing a bomber squadron's combat box. As the pilots banked and turned to evade the incoming weapons, the Luftwaffe fighters learned to pounce before the Americans could get back in formation.

A smoke pot marks the bomb release point for a formation of B-24 Liberators during a mission over France in June 1944. The days of individual bombardiers taking aim on a target were long gone and so was the illusion of pinpoint bombing.

Wrestling command of the air from the Luftwaffe did not come cheap.

Hermann Goering continued to lose credibility with Hitler as the Luftwaffe's ability to perform its roles declined. In turn, he castigated his fighter leaders and questioned their bravery at a time when the front-line units were being pushed to the breaking point by the Allied air offensive.

Watchful eyes peer out from above the oxygen mask. Captain Oscar O'Neil, pilot and plane commander of a B-17 named *Invasion II*, personifies the veteran's sense of vigilance in combat.

infrastructure. The new effort began on May 12 when the Eighth hit seven synthetic oil plants with almost a thousand bombers. The Germans reacted fiercely, shooting down forty-six bombers while losing fifty-six interceptor pilots killed and wounded.

The bombing was not incredibly accurate, but one plant lost 17 percent of its production capacity. Albert Speer, Hitler's Minister of Armaments, reacted to the Eighth Air Force's raids with extreme alarm. He wrote Hitler, "The enemy has struck us at one of our weakest points. If they persist . . . we will soon no longer have any fuel production worth mentioning."

The gravity of the situation forced the Germans to redeploy their anti-aircraft defenses to better protect the oil industry. By the fall of 1944, over a thousand AA guns protected key

For two years, the Americans and British had executed amphibious landings in both the Pacific and Mediterranean theaters. The hard-won lessons learned from those earlier operations were absorbed and incorporated into Operation Overlord, the invasion of western France. The key in every instance: command of the air over the beaches.

American troops load up for D-Day in Southampton Harbor.

While Harris and some other strategic-minded air commanders believed the diversion of the heavies in support of the pre-invasion aerial operations over France was a wasteful diversion from the main mission of crushing Germany's industries and morale, the fact was using the strategic forces saved the lives of countless soldiers and sailors who otherwise would have faced much more intense opposition. Scenes like this sinking LCI would have been far more common had the Luftwaffe been able to strike the beachhead in numbers.

The final softening up aerial bombardment before the D-Day landings including Ninth Air Force B-26 Marauders hammering Utah Beach and the Eighth Air Force pounding targets behind Omaha Beach.

The crucial moments: Vulnerable LCVPs like this one churn for the Normandy shore, June 6, 1944.

A formation of Liberators on their bomb run.

installations. These were not facilities that could be moved underground. Since the beginning of the year, the Germans had been busy establishing critical factories in mines and gigantic underground complexes to make them impervious to bombing. Much of the aircraft industry had been reorganized this way, and slave laborers from concentration camps were used on the production lines. In this way, Speer was able to drastically increase the outflow of armaments and aircraft despite all the damage the Allied air forces were doing to Germany's cities.

Oil turned out to be the Reich's Achilles' heel. Cracking plants and refineries could not be moved underground or hardened. The only thing the Germans could do was ring them with anti-aircraft guns and trust that the Luftwaffe could hinder the attacking bombers.

The Luftwaffe could not. At the end of the month, Spaatz hammered the oil targets again. This time using four hundred bombers, thirty-two of which went down, the accuracy was stunning. The attacks inflicted massive damage. Combined with several Fifteenth Air Force raids on Ploesti, Spaatz's bombers cut German oil production in half by the end of May. Despite losing eighty-four B-17s and B-24s, plus almost 850 airmen, the Americans had scored the biggest victory yet in the strategic air war.

All day long on the 6th, the VIII Fighter Command flew missions in support of the amphibious landings. Here, a 361st Fighter Group P-51 gets the signal for take-off in the morning. Some of the VIII's pilots flew three missions or more that day.

In the month before D-Day, with the transportation plan fully executed, the Eighth and Fifteenth Air Forces struck at oil targets all over Central and Eastern Europe. The Fifteenth concentrated on Ploesti. Long gone were the days where the USAAF dreamed of a single, knockout blow on that critical facility. Instead, a grim campaign between the American bombers and the Axis repair crews played out through the spring and summer of 1944. The Fifteenth struck Ploesti scores of times, inflicting massive damage. Yet, in the end production didn't cease until the first Russian tanks rolled through the refineries later in 1944.

Hunted on the ground, chased until flamed in the air, the Luftwaffe's once-vaunted strength ebbed away to a skeletal presence by the end of the summer of 1944.

Return of the 361st Fighter Group following a mission over Normandy. The fighters of the Mighty Eighth ensured the Germans paid in spades for moving troops, supplies, or vehicles in daylight toward the growing battle in western France.

As the Luftwaffe's interceptors were swept from the skies, the Germans increasingly relied on anti-aircraft batteries for their nation's defense. It was a rare day over Germany when a bomb group could return without anti-aircraft artillery damage to its aircraft.

The destruction of Germany's above-ground military industries continued through the summer, even after the shift to oil targets took place. Here, a thoroughly bombed Panther tank factory is examined after the war by curious GIs.

The German war machine felt the new campaign's effects immediately. Calls went out to every command to conserve fuel and oil. Ruthless economy measures were put in place. The training of new pilots suffered as less aviation gas was made available. That meant the cadets received fewer hours in the air before being flung against the bomber streams. Worse things would soon follow as the campaign gained momentum.

May saw the first decline in American heavy bomber losses since the daylight strategic campaign began almost two years before. Not only did the USAAF have more Forts and Liberators available than any other time, the Luftwaffe had been ground down so severely by the attritional warfare over the Reich that its fighter units were staffed now by an increasingly small number of old hands surrounded by half-trained replacements. Since March, the battles over Germany had cost the Reich defense units no fewer than twenty-eight aces killed in

As the Allied armies advanced into France, they came across some curious sights. Here in this ruined hangar the troops discovered a captured 100th Bomb Group B-17 Flying Fortress.

A 305th Bomb Group B-17 burns after crash-landing in France. The Allied advance in Western Europe afforded the Eighth Air Force new emergency airfields to use in case of battle damage. Thousands of airmen owed their lives to the front's eastward shift that summer and fall.

A Fort crew prepares for a crash-landing.

By the summer of 1944, the B-17 ruled supreme in Germany's daylight skies.

action. Others, like Gunther Rall, suffered wounds that would keep them out of the fight for weeks and months to come.

The Luftwaffe started the year with 2,395 single-engine fighter pilots. By June 1, 1944, the jagdgeschwaders had lost 2,262 of those pilots. In six months, the Luftwaffe suffered almost 100 percent losses. No organization can survive such a body blow. That the survivors continued to intercept raids and at times inflict heavy casualties stands as a testament to the courage and dedication in the face of an increasingly obvious lost cause.

In June, the Allied heavy bombers worked in concert with the rest of the D-Day invasion force to pummel the Germans in their coastal emplacements. After two weeks of that, Spaatz returned to the oil industry targets and began crossing them off a list that totaled slightly under a hundred facilities. In between raids, Bomber Command and the Eighth were both used as battlefield sledgehammers in Normandy in hopes of breaking the deadlock there. The Eighth nearly destroyed the elite Panzer Lehr Division around St. Lo in a carpet bombing attack that also inflicted almost five hundred friendly casualties on forward American units.

Despite the commitments in Normandy, Spaatz's raids on the oil targets continued. By now, the Germans were experts in on-the-fly fix-it industrial repair. Workers swarmed over these critical facilities and soon restored much of the lost production. This time, Spaatz gave them no respite. Gone were the days of the single knock-out blow. The Americans had come up their learning curve and understood to win this campaign would require tenacity, patience, and consistency. By the end of July, the Eighth and Fifteenth smothered the aviation fuel facilities with hundreds of tons of bombs, reducing output by 98 percent. Speer's apocalyptic vision of what lay ahead for the Reich had come true.

A V-1 plunges into a crowded London neighborhood.

14

CLUTCHING STRAWS

"The superstition of the wonder weapon struck me as a transparent trick."
—*Johannes Steinhoff,* In Letzter Stunde

THEY WERE SUPPOSED TO SAVE THE THIRD REICH: new technologies that seemingly came straight off the pages of pulp magazines and comic books. Rockets, guided missiles and jet fighters—the Germans raced the clock in a frantic effort to field these new "wonder weapons" that Hitler hoped would turn the tide of the war.

Offensively, the new weapons included the V-1 "Buzz Bomb" and the V-2 rocket. Both were used against London, Antwerp, and targets in Southern England. The V-1 became the world's first operational cruise missile on June 13, 1944, when the Germans fired an initial volley at Southern England from facilities in France and Holland. With a 1,870-pound warhead, the V-1 could fly about 250 miles at 400 miles an hour.

Using a primitive autopilot system linked to a vane anemometer, the V-1 would fly in the general direction of its target. Once it traveled the distance between its launch ramp back and its intended destination, it would automatically enter a steep dive and explode on impact with the ground.

From June until the end of the war, the Germans launched about 9,500 "Doodle Bugs" at Allied targets. Only a quarter of those made it anywhere near their destination. Barrage balloons, anti-aircraft defenses, and fighters accounted for thousands of them. The others strayed off course or crashed. Still, the relatively small number that did reach their targets did considerable damage. By war's end, the V-1 menace had killed or wounded over twenty-one thousand civilians.

The last German terror campaign used weapons straight from the pulp comic books of the era. The V-1 pilotless "buzz bomb" was the first of these new devices designed to kill civilians indiscriminately from remote locations hundreds of miles away.

The V-2 proved to be a much more menacing and dangerous weapon. The world's first ballistic missile, the V-2 actually entered sub-orbital flight on its trajectory to its target area. First launched against England on September 8, 1944, the V-2 alarmed Churchill and the rest of his cabinet. It flew too fast to be detected, prepared against, or shot down. In fact, most of the time it would impact and explode before anyone had heard it.

The launch pads could not be bombed, either, as the V-1s could. The V-2 could be carted around by trucks and fired from almost anywhere. Trying to knock out their facilities would simply not work. There were no defenses for such a weapon—that would have to wait decades until the advent of anti-ballistic missile systems.

The people of London and Antwerp would just have to endure. The mysterious explosions that rocked the British capital that fall were initially brushed off as gas leaks by the government, which sought to avoid a panic over the new weapon wielded against the civilian population.

A British Tempest chases a V-1 across the English countryside.

To produce the Reich's "wonder weapons" required setting up underground factories that could not be destroyed by Allied bombs. Here, GIs check out a V-1 production line in an underground facility after the war.

The dreaded V-2, the world's first operational ballistic missile. The Allies possessed no defense to such a weapon and had to rely on counterintelligence tricks to fool the Germans as to the accuracy and lethality of their new weapon. This one was photographed in the United States after the war during a testing operation.

V-2 strikes inflicted about three thousand casualties and scored some horrifying hits on crowded locations. In Antwerp, 537 people died when a V-2 struck a movie theater. Another one landed on a Woolworth's in London, killing 108.

With no effective defense, the British resorted to trickery. The Germans had developed a radio beam guidance system that gave the V-2 effective accuracy. Using its intelligence network, the British fed the Germans false information that the V-2s were falling ten to twenty miles beyond London. The Germans fell for this completely, recalibrated their guidance system and after that most of the V-2s fell harmlessly into the Kent countryside.

The V-1 and V-2 programs absorbed enough German industrial resources and material to produce an estimated twenty-four thousand fighters. In the end, they achieved nothing more beyond senseless destruction and loss of civilian life. Yet, these two offensive vengeance weapons gave hope to the besieged German people, whose sufferings under Allied bombs sparked a desire for revenge. The V-1 and V-2 attacks satisfied that urge. In a real sense, the Nazi regime invested vast treasure and resources into these weapons to mollify the population and inspire continued support for the government and the war effort. In the end, the average V-2 strike killed two people. The payoff did not match the outlay.

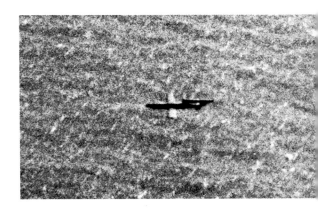

A buzz bomb over the English Channel. The V-1 threat forced the Allies to devote fighter units to anti–buzz bomb defense. Shooting them down required speed and nerve. Sometimes, the pilots would actually fly alongside them and use a wing tip to flip the buzz bomb over, causing it to lose control and crash.

Coinciding with this mini-blitz on London was the arrival of the Messerschmitt 262 in operational service. The world's first jet aircraft to reach front line units, the Me-262 symbolized the Luftwaffe's last, best hope to turn the tide in the skies over the Reich. After the war, so much misinformation and outright lies about the aircraft circulated in the memoirs of various Luftwaffe leaders that for decades the true nature of this revolutionary weapon has been clouded. Fortunately a new crop of historians, led by Manfred Boehme, have stripped away much of the myth.

THE PEOPLE'S WONDER WEAPON

WITH THE SHORTAGE of fighter pilots reaching a crisis point, Goering and Speer concocted a scheme to redress the situation. What if a new jet fighter could be built from non-strategic materials and was easy enough to fly that Hitler Youth members could pilot it into battle with minimal training?

Galland thought this scheme ridiculous. He advocated throwing all the production resources possible into the Me-262 program. Goering and Speer overruled him. The "People's Fighter" would go forward.

The Heinkel He-162 was the result of this delusional and desperate vision. At the end of September 1944, Goering gave the green light to the He-162. Heinkel went to work constructing a prototype built of wood and glued together. Rapid progress was made until the RAF bombed the glue factory that produced what the He-162 needed. The substitute found failed repeatedly and caused a wing to come off during the aircraft's second flight in December. Nevertheless, the Heinkel was thrown into production, flaws and all.

The first forty-six were sent to an operational test unit in January 1945. The "Salamander," as the He-162 was called, turned out to be a tricky plane to fly. This made the idea of using Hitler Youth teenagers, versed only in glider flying, to pilot these new aircraft a preposterous proposition.

In the early spring, elements of JG-1 received the He-162 and began flying it operationally. Powered by the BMW-003 turbojet engine rejected for use in the ME-262 program, the Salamander could sustain speeds of over five hundred miles per

hour, though it had a combat flying time of only thirty minutes. Worse, the BMW engine tended to flame out, and at least ten He-162s crashed in accidents. Altogether, about 120 reached combat squadrons. A few kills were scored in the final air battles of the war. Two He-162s were lost in return. When the Allies finally overran the Heinkel factories, they discovered hundreds of He-162s awaiting delivery. Altogether, about six hundred rolled off production lines before the war ended.

The Heinkel He-162 Salamander was born from desperation at the pilot attrition rate suffered by the Luftwaffe's interceptor force. Initially, it was supposed to be flown by half-trained teenagers recruited from Hitler Youth organizations. In practice, the He-162 required a highly trained pilot to fly.

The Me-262's genesis dates back to April 1939 when Messerschmitt produced the first plans for a twin-engined jet fighter. The following year, on November 1, 1940, Messerschmitt went to work on the new design, now dubbed "Project III." The initial airframe rolled out of the factory in January 1941. Later that spring, the project's engineers fitted a conventional piston engine to the aircraft's nose and test flew it for the first time. After numerous modifications, the first pure jet version of the new aircraft took flight a year later in July 1942.

The Me-262 represented a quantum technological leap over existing aeronautical technology. Like all major leaps forward, the project encountered numerous problems, not

By the summer of 1944, the Luftwaffe's fighter force was equipped with increasingly obsolescent aircraft like the Bf-109. Eclipsed by planes such as the Mustang, the Spitfire XIV, the Hawker Tempest, and other Allied aircraft, the already hopelessly outnumbered German fighter pilots no longer stood a chance in the skies over Europe in the aircraft available to them. Adolf Galland, Goering, and others pinned their slender hopes on the revolutionary new Me-262 jet fighter-bomber. A hundred miles an hour faster than the P-51, Galland saw it as the weapon that could wrest control of the air away from the Allies and save Germany's cities from further destruction.

An American patrol comes across a Me-262 in Austria. German jet technology became one of the most sought-after prizes in the postwar. Both the Russians and the Americans scoured the remains of the Reich to locate those who conceived and tried to perfect the 262 and other "wonder weapons."

the least of which were the unreliable BMW jet engines. By 1942, Germany faced a crushing shortage of strategic materials, which made producing the complex metal alloys that could withstand the super-heated environment within a jet engine feasible. Substitutes for such parts had to be found, and all had serious drawbacks. The BMW engines never fully matured and the Me-262 program switched to the Junkers Jumo 004. The change helped only slightly. The Junkers contained the same Achilles' heel the BMW engines possessed and could only function for about a dozen flight hours before they needed replacement.

The technical problems surrounding the engines delayed the Me-262's development throughout its gestational phase. In 1943, Adolf Galland flew one of the prototypes and saw the future from its cockpit. He saw this aircraft as the solution to the growing Allied strategic bombing campaign. With a fighter arm equipped with Me-262s, he believed the Luftwaffe could sweep the skies clear of Allied planes. He pushed for its immediate introduction.

That couldn't happen any time soon. Teething troubles continued to plague the Me-262 and its engines. Messerschmitt announced in June 1943 that January 1944 would be the earliest it could deliver the first pre-production versions. Production would follow by the summer. Messerschmitt intended to construct 430 Me-262s a month by October 1944.

When the 262 showed up in the skies over Germany in the fall of 1944, the new fighter sent shock waves through the USAAF. Careful analysis of the jet's performance helped mitigate its speed advantage. Mustang and Thunderbolt pilots learned that the 262 could not hope to maneuver with their more nimble fighters. The 262 was an energy fighter—fast passes and quick disengagements were the tactics needed for it to be successful. If a Messerschmitt pilot attempted air combat maneuvering, he would mostly likely end up going down in flames.

The 262's engines could not be throttled up quickly, making them sluggish to accelerate. The Mustangs and Thunderbolts capitalized on that weakness by camping over airfields used by 262s and picking them off at their most vulnerable moments, as the jets began to take off or came in to land.

In the war's final weeks, a two-seat night fighter version of the Me-262 began arriving from Messerschmitt's underground production lines. It could have been a very effective addition to the nacht jaeger units, but it did not reach operational service in numbers. Besides, the ground war was all but over.

Walter Nowotny, one of Germany's leading aces, took command of one of the first 262 fighter units. He led it into combat and was killed while fighting the Eighth Air Force in one of the new jets.

After the war, bitter Luftwaffe leaders like Adolf Galland sought to present the 262 as a potential tide-turning weapon that could have resulted in a German victory. But political bungling on Hitler's part doomed the 262 and caused so many delays that it didn't reach operational service until too late. Pure fiction. The 262 program was fraught with technological and material issues that took time to overcome. Even when it did reach operational status, the 262 represented immature technology that presented many very serious problems and limited its effectiveness in combat.

After the war, Adolf Galland, Albert Speer, and other senior leaders within the Luftwaffe and Third Reich claimed that Hitler repeatedly intervened in the Me-262 in such a chaotic manner that he delayed its introduction by months, if not years. They found a perfect scapegoat for the Luftwaffe's defeat: a globally reviled dead madman whom nobody would ever defend. As a result, the early postwar literature is colored with this blame-laying and legend-spinning.

The legend goes like this: Hitler saw in the Me-262 its offensive potential and in 1943 ordered it to be produced as a bomber. That decision cost the program months as modifications were necessary to carry out the Fuehrer's orders. Additionally, Galland claimed that Hitler ordered Messerschmitt not to prepare for full series production of the Me-262.

First, the Me-262 was designed to be a fighter-bomber virtually since its inception. Hanging a couple of bombs under the wings did not require the massive redesign the apologists

When attacking bomber formations, the Me-262 pilots generally attacked from astern and used rockets first before closing to cannon range. The four 30mm guns in the nose could tear apart a Fort or B-24 with just a handful of hits. Here, a B-24 goes down as two members of its crew free fall clear of it.

The Me-163 was a deadly aviation design Hail Mary—deadly for its pilots. A rocket fighter with only a few minutes' fuel supply, it was supposed to engage the bomber stream, glide back to its airfield, and land on a centerline skid. In tests, landings often resulted in the Me-163 blowing up or, even worse. the fuel tanks rupturing and pouring toxic chemicals into the cockpit that would essentially melt the pilot.

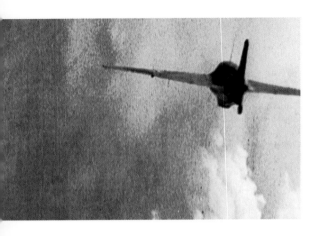

With a top speed of over six hundred miles per hour, the Me-163 was all but impossible to intercept for a P-51 or Thunderbolt. However, once it burned through its small fuel load, the pilot now found himself in a modern air war at the controls of a glider. Within weeks of the end of the war, the 163 program was cancelled and the remaining pilots sent to Me-262 units.

German rocket and missile technology was far ahead of any Allied program. This weapon was the X-4, a wire-guided surface-to-air missile designed to be directed to a bomber stream where its proximity fuse would detonate its warhead. It did not see operational service, but could have been a deadly effective weapon.

have argued. And production was not hampered by Hitler's decision-making, it was delayed by technical troubles, lack of engines and material, and the chaotic state of the Reich as a result of the strategic bombing campaign.

The fact that the first Me-262s reached experimental units in the summer of 1944 was akin to a miracle, one that symbolized the remarkable capacity of the German aviation industry. Despite all manners of hardship, not the least of which most of Messerschmitt's prewar factories burned to the ground in the wake of Allied bombing raids, the Me-262 reached operational status and made aviation history.

In July, nine Me-262 from Kommando Schenk moved to France to begin high-altitude bombing missions against the Allies in Normandy. Two months later, elements of KG-51 began to re-equip with the jet aircraft, though the numbers available remained paltry.

While a few Me-262 were diverted to the Luftwaffe's bomber force, Kommando Hauptmann Werner Thierfelder had been preparing to take it into battle since December 1943. Once again, aircraft and engines served as the limiting factor. In the summer, Thierfelder died and Walter Nowotny took over the unit. It was renamed after him and sent into the fray to defend the Reich from American daylight bombers.

By fall, the situation for the Luftwaffe's fighter force had grown beyond desperate. Half-trained pilots, thrown into the air in now-obsolescent aircraft like the Bf-109 died with grim rapidity. The average Luftwaffe fighter pilot died in combat after eight to thirty days of operational service. The last few remaining veteran leaders and aces attempted to hold things

together as best they could, but the fresh-faced replacements they received possessed less than a hundred hours of total flying time. There wasn't much they could do to save them. The learning curve in the skies over the Reich proved far too steep. Of the 107 Luftwaffe aces to score a hundred or more kills, only 8 of them joined fighter units after the summer of 1942. The rest were the old hands who formed the backbone of an increasingly brittle and green force.

The Luftwaffe's leadership deluded itself believing that the Me-262 could change this dynamic and restore air superiority over the Third Reich. They pinned their hopes to the wrong star. Rushed into service, the Me-262 units suffered high casualty rates from operational accidents. The pilots were not well-trained on the revolutionary new aircraft. The engines failed and sometimes caught fire in flight. The operational attrition rate stayed high,

While the wonder weapons received most of Goebbels's ink, other firms, like Dornier, went to work on making the most out of existing technology. The Dornier-335 Arrow was the product of this design avenue. Powered by a pusher and tractor engine both, it possessed surprising speed and agility for such a large aircraft. Its two-seat version would have been a very capable night fighter. Very few were constructed during the chaotic final weeks of the war, and the program had no impact on the fighting.

FOR MOST OF WORLD WAR II, THE SS pervaded nearly every aspect of the Nazi war machine. The one place that had been out of bounds was Goering's Luftwaffe. As the strategic bombing campaign forced Germany to look for increasingly desperate solutions to their air defense issues, Bachem came up with a hybrid aircraft/missile called the Ba-349 Natter. The

Germans had been working on surface-to-air missile technology, but could not get the guidance system or the proximity fuses to work properly. A pilot seemed like the obvious solution to that problem. That was the concept behind the Natter. Powered by a rocket engine plus four supplementary JATO-like rockets designed to be jettisoned after launch, the Natter would be

The Bachem Ba-349 Natter was conceived as a sort of man-directed surface-to-air missile and was supposed to have been a cheap way to hit Allied bomber formations.

guided to a passing bomber stream by a ground controller. Once at the proper altitude, all the pilot had to do was pitch the nose forward, ditch the plastic nosecone to unmask a hive of two dozen or more air-to-air unguided rockets. The pilot would salvo them into the bomber stream then eject from the Natter's cockpit.

Head of the SS Heinrich Himmler took an interest in the project and made available the funds to build the weapon. Thirty-six eventually were constructed. A manned flight test actually took place in March 1945. One of the booster rockets failed to release, which threw the Natter out of control. The test pilot attempted to bail out after releasing the canopy. He failed to escape from the craft and went down with the craft to his death. There is some speculation that as it plummeted to earth, the Natter broke the speed of sound.

After the war, the USAAF captured four Natters and test fired one (without a pilot) at Muroc Field in 1946.

The Natter attracted the interest of Heinrich Himmler, head of the SS. He liked the concept so much that he funded it with SS money.

In theory, the Natter pilot would ride his rocket up to the Allied bomber stream, level out long enough to fire a nose full of unguided missiles into the formations, then eject from the Natter and float back to earth in a parachute.

There was only one manned test launch before the end of the war. It did not go well, and the pilot was killed when the Natter swung out of control and crashed.

and losses in combat with the USAAF ran to 15 percent. Late in the war, in one air battle, the Me-262 units suffered 56 percent casualties trying to defend the Reich.

For all these difficulties, the Me-262 certainly had potential. Though it could not accelerate quickly due to the nature of its engines, it possessed a top speed of almost 540 miles per hour—100 miles an hour quicker than the Spitfire or Mustang. Armed with four bomber-killing 30mm cannon plus twenty-four air-to-air rockets, The Me-262 solved the firepower problem that plagued the Bf-109 and Fw-190 geschwaders. Finally, the Luftwaffe could wield a bomber-destroyer that, unlike the Bf-110 or 410, could defend itself against fighter attacks thanks to its superior speed.

The Luftwaffe banked on it to save the day—and the night. The RAF continued its relentless destruction of Germany's major cities. Casualties remained heavy, though the advent of Mosquito night fighters to escort the bombers helped keep the losses manageable. Aside from the Heinkel-219, the Germans did not have a night fighter anywhere near as fast and maneuverable as the Mossie.

Toward war's end, a two-seat variant equipped with the latest "Stag Antler" airborne radar system began to roll off the production lines. Nachtgeschwader I received a few of these aircraft along with some standard single-seat Me-262s. For three months, they flew against the RAF and demonstrated the new jet's dominance over the sleek and fast Mosquitoes.

The bomber kampfgeschwaders were to receive their own new jet attack aircraft in 1944–1945. This was the Arado-234. Faster than any Allied fighter, it could operate almost entirely free of threat of interception.

The advent of the jet fighter over Germany caused a ripple of panic in the USAAF that reached all the way back to Washington, D.C. Arnold, Spaatz, and Doolittle feared the Germans might actually be able to stop the combined bomber offensive if they could field enough Me-262s.

While the Allies kicked their own jet fighter programs into high gear, the front line P-51 and P-47 units devised tactics to counter the Me-262's incredible speed advantage. The jet's Achilles' heel lay in its inability to accelerate quickly. The Americans picked up on this and concluded the best place to strike back at the jets—which the VIII Fighter Command pilots irreverently called "blowjobs"—was over their home airfields as they landed or took off.

The remains of a prototype space-age weapon known as the Gotha Go-229. This radical design presaged the American flying wing and B-2 Spirit programs by years. The project did not go far, but in concept the Go-229 would have been a tail-less, bat-shaped fighter-interceptor capable of speeds in excess of six hundred miles per hour.

As the Germans threw new technology into the fray, the Americans relied on the tried and true, first created in the 1930s. Here, an Eighth Air Force bombardier sits in the nose of his B-17G. The Norden sight was used to aim ordnance on German targets right until the final days of the war.

A B-24's waist gunner. Though technology and new designs affected the ebb and flow of the air campaign, at its roots the experience over Europe during World War II was a very human and tragic one.

Down low and slow, the 262 was fresh meat for enterprising American pilots. When Me-262s hit an American formation, the escort fighters would immediately dispatch roving flights to all the nearby airdromes with concrete runways in hopes of catching the 262s in their most vulnerable moments.

On October 7, 1944, Kommando Nowotny prepared to intercept 1,300 Eighth Air Force bombers en route to raid Germany's oil infrastructure. Their home airfield at Achmer attracted the attention of a formation of 361st Fighter Group P-51s. Urban Drew spotted a couple of Me-262s on the runway. As they took off, he rolled into a dive from fifteen thousand feet and caught the trailing jet just after it tucked in its landing gear. With the 262 barely going two hundred miles per hour, Drew closed quickly and shot it out of the sky. The lead jet tried to get away by executing a climbing left turn, but Drew had energy and speed to burn after his 14,000 foot dive. He caught up to the other jet and raked it with .50-caliber bullets until it flipped over and augered into the ground.

Such attacks claimed the lives of several Kommando Nowotny pilots. On November 8, 1944, after his unit had been visited by several irate Luftwaffe generals who castigated the pilots for losing their fighting edge, Nowotny climbed into a 262 and set off to intercept an American B-24 formation.

Nowotny was one of the last "great" Luftwaffe aces. He held the Knight's Cross and had been credited with 256 kills. Along with several other 262s from his unit, he struck the Liberator boxes outside of Achmer, shot one down and claimed a P-51. Moments later, he radioed back to base that he was on fire. His jet plummeted through a layer of clouds and cratered a few miles from his unit's runway. The exact cause of his death cannot be established. He was either shot down by P-51s or he suffered one of the common and catastrophic engine fires so common to the immature technology embedded in the 262's design.

Limping home with wounded aboard, an Eighth Air Force B-17 fires distress flares on final approach so the ambulance and fire crews can rush to their assistance.

Planning for the day's mission.

If the Me-262 was barely operationally ready in the fall of 1944, the Luftwaffe killed a lot of its own pilots by sending the Messerschmitt Me-163 "Komet" into battle. Designed as a short-ranged, rocket powered point defense fighter, the tiny Komet carried two 30mm cannons and could reach sustained speeds of over six hundred miles an hour. It was the fastest thing in the sky that year, and when its blowtorch was burning, no Allied fighter could touch it.

Yet, major drawbacks abounded. First, the rocket engine carried only enough fuel for about fifteen minutes of use. Canny Me-163 pilots would milk their fuel load by shutting the rocket off and gliding once they'd climbed above the bomber formation they had intercepted. Coasting along, they'd pick their target, restart the rocket and swoop down for a rear attack. Once they'd burned through their 120 cannon shells, they'd dive away and out of the fight. Then they'd glide back to their runway to make a landing on the narrow centerline skid.

Jagdgeschwader 400 flew the Me-163 in combat, claiming around a dozen kills while losing about the same number of aircraft operationally and in combat. Though the aircraft's speed was unmatched and it could climb to 39,000 feet in an astonishing three minutes, the Komet failed as a bomber destroyer. The closure rate between an Me-163 and a B-17 was so great that the gunnery runs the Luftwaffe pilots could make lasted only a couple of seconds, even with a rear attack. The 30mm cannon was slow firing and had a low muzzle velocity, making it difficult for a 163 pilot to score a kill shot on a B-17 or B-24.

The fuel used to power the rocket engine was extremely caustic. In some instances, pilots returning after a flight would land hard on the skid and rupture one of the tanks, sending deadly chemicals into the Komet's cockpit with gruesome results. As a result, the Me-163 drivers wore unique flight suits made of asbestos to prevent them from a horrible death.

The bomber crews were frequently overburdened with bulky flight suits and armor designed to protect them from the freezing temperatures and flak shrapnel. Moving around while in the air came with only great effort.

A bomb-ravaged Dornier factory rusts in postwar Germany, the remains of a Dornier-335 still sitting in the old production area.

Despite the arrival of the Me-262, the Mustang remained the dominate presence over Europe throughout 1944–1945.

In the final weeks of the war, the Luftwaffe recognized the Me-163's failure and disbanded JG-400. Its surviving pilots joined Me-262 units and served out the war in the more effective, if still troubled, twin-engined jet.

The wonder weapons may have put a scare into the Allies in the final months of the war, but ultimately none of them had any effect on the Third Reich's fate. In the air, the tiny number of Me-262s that rose to challenge the thousands of Allied bombers were simply brushed aside. As Spaatz's men continued to hammer oil targets, the Reich all but ran out of fuel by the end of 1944.

Come winter, there were hardly any worthwhile urban targets left in Germany to bomb. The combined offensive had left the Reich in utter ruin, its people "dehoused," their industries and neighborhoods destroyed. By early 1945, the bombs dropped during further area attacks just rearranged the rubble. In the war's final months, Bomber Command dropped 181,000 tons of ordnance on Germany. So many bombs were expended that the factories back in England could not keep pace with the demand, and shortages plagued the RAF for the war's final weeks.

Germany lay in ruins. Still its military and people fought on until the bitter end. And bitter it was. On February 13–14, 1945, Bomber Command sent aloft two waves of Mossies, Lancs, and Halifaxes, all bound for the picturesque city of Dresden, some 770 miles from England. The first wave carried 4,000-pound blockbuster bombs, designed to destroy water and sewer mains with their fearsome blasts, along with some two hundred thousand incendiaries.

Flying at 8,000 feet, the first wave of 250 Lancasters dropped all their ordnance on Dresden in under ten minutes. A firestorm took shape within the one-square-mile target area, sending flames so high that the second wave could see the city from sixty miles away.

The second wave was specifically intended to kill or incapacitate the rescue and fire crews fighting to save the city. Three hours after the first raid, the second one arrived and sowed even more destruction. Within minutes, the RAF bombers ravaged the city with another 1,800 tons of bombs.

The firestorm sent smoke up 15,000 feet. Temperatures reached 1,800 degrees. The civilians caught in the inferno were burned alive or died of smoke inhalation or asphyxiation when the firestorm sucked the oxygen out of their shelters. Others tried to flee the growing conflagration, but the flames sucked the air right out of the streets as well. Those who could not get away fast enough would suddenly fall unconscious, victims of anoxia. Seconds later, the flames would burn them to ashes.

The next morning, four hundred Flying Forts from the Eighth Air Force's First Bomb Division struck Dresden as the dazed survivors dug themselves out of the rubble. The Eighth returned on February 15 to rearrange the rubble. Fires still blazed everywhere, and the dead lay untended in the firestorm's wake. Somewhere between twenty-one thousand and forty thousand people died during these attacks. Over six thousand were cremated in one of the city squares, a testament to the desperate nature of the post-attack circumstances. Rescue and clean-up crews stumbled across so many bodies partially burned in shelters that eventually they gave up trying to extricate them. Instead, they cremated them in place with flamethrowers.

Seventy-eight thousand buildings lay destroyed, including most of Dresden's industrial plants. Since the war, Dresden's military value and the importance of its factories to the Third Reich's war machine have been questioned by succeeding generations of historians. Some have called the Dresden raids a war crime. Debate rages over it even today.

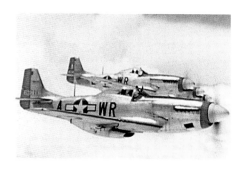

355th Fighter Group P-51s. By the end of 1944, almost all the Eighth Air Force units had converted to the Mustang. The notable exception was the 56th Fighter Group, which loved its Jugs.

A common sight in early 1945 were hundreds upon hundreds of B-17s, all in tight combat box formations, streaming across Germany to deal destruction to numerous targets a day.

The suffering of those on the ground whose cities were destroyed by Allied bombs cannot lightly be dismissed. The February raids on Dresden have continued to arouse moral repulsion and have sparked ethical debates on the entire concept of strategic bombing ever since.

Singling out one raid seems at best an intellectual exercise when the bombing campaign killed up to 650,000 German civilians during the war. The Royal Air Force's area bombing attacks claimed two-thirds of those lives. Other cities—Rostock and Hamburg among them—suffered Dresden's fate.

As the Luftwaffe ran out of fuel, replacement aircraft, and pilots, it became impossible for its fighter units to contest every raid. Instead, during the final weeks of the war, the jagdgruppen would husband their resources until they had enough planes and gasoline to put a substantial force aloft. While they sometimes could score isolated successes, the inexperienced Luftwaffe pilots fell in droves to their better-trained veteran opponents in the Eighth and Fifteenth Air Forces.

As the Soviet army advanced on Berlin, the bombing campaign wound down. The last RAF raid on Berlin took place on April 21–22, 1945. A few days later, Bomber Command flew its final major mission. This final raid took out an oil refinery in Norway. The Eighth Air Force ran out of targets at the end of April as well. After repeated fighter sweeps and ground attack missions destroyed almost a thousand German aircraft in the air and on the ground, the heavy bombers hit the Skoda Armaments complex in Czechoslovakia on April 25. After that, the Eighth stood down. Mission accomplished.

The Third Reich's cities had been destroyed. Germany's industrial base had been ground to dust. The Luftwaffe had first been shot out of the sky, then hunted to extinction on the ground. Around 90 percent of Germany's single engine fighter pilots became casualties during the war. Those were Stalingrad odds.

In return, Bomber Command suffered a 76 percent casualty rate. A young British male had a better chance of survival in the trenches of the Western Front as an infantry officer than he did in the skies over Germany.

The Eighth Air Force lost 49,000 airmen out of 350,000 deployed to East Anglia during the war. Altogether, the combined air offensive had cost the Allies over 100,000 men.

Hardly had the ink dried on Germany's surrender document when the second guessing began. Given all the destruction, all the deaths of airmen and civilians, was the strategic bombing worth the effort?

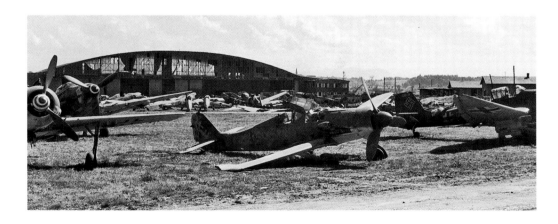

The shattered aftermath of the German war machine.

While historians have debated the morality of the bombing campaign as well as its effectiveness, nobody disputes that the early 1944 USAAF campaign dealt the crippling blows that ultimately defeated the Luftwaffe over its own home turf.

Epilogue

JUDGMENTS

"We cut our way through a basement wall to discover a reeking hash of over 100 human beings. Flame must have swept through before the building's collapse sealed the exits, because the flesh of those within resembled the texture of prunes. Our job, it was explained, was to wade into the shambles and bring forth the remains. Encouraged by cuffing and guttural abuse, wade in we did. We did exactly that, for the floor was covered with an unsavoury broth from burst water mains and viscera."

—*Kurt Vonnegut on his experiences in Dresden.* Armageddon in Retrospect

THE AIRPOWER THEORISTS WERE WRONG. Instead of avoiding the horrific attritional battles like the Somme and Verdun by striking quick, decisive blows from the air, strategic bombing ultimately became World War II's aerial version of the Western Front. It consumed men and machines at a rate no other service endured. By 1943, the "quick war" solution airpower seemingly offered in the eyes of Mitchell or Douhet was clearly never going to materialize. The one-raid wonder missions designed to deliver a knock-out punch at a vital industry simply did not work. Ploesti proved that. So did Regensburg and Schweinfurt. The postwar U.S. Strategic Bombing Survey concluded, "The German experience showed that, whatever the target system, no indispensable industry was permanently put out of commission by a single attack. Persistent re-attack was necessary."

This essential truth about waging war on industries that could be repaired or rebuilt set the table for the massive attritional campaigns of 1944-45.

Douhet's belief that an enemy could be forced to surrender by crushing civilian morale formed the centerpiece of Sir Arthur Harris's vision for Bomber Command's nocturnal raids on Germany. Five years of bombing never produced a peoples' uprising, as Douhet believed would happen. Germany's will to keep fighting never wavered until Red Army boots set foot in the Reichstag in the final days of the Battle of Berlin. Sir Arthur Harris, Portal, and the crews of Bomber Command waged a five-year war on civilian morale, in part because the British had no other way to sustain an offensive against Germany. It never paid off with the decisive victory Harris sought, but it clearly affected the Nazi hierarchy's decision making process,

Bomber Harris, a devoted Douhetist and single-minded believer in the strategic air war.

For five years, Europe's cities had been ravaged by aerial bombing. In the process, tens of thousands of men had perished in the flak- and fighter-filled skies. Below these raging air battles, more than six hundred thousand civilians died in firestorms and explosions or were crushed by falling debris. Incendiaries melted them as they fled, and others died of anoxia when the boiling flames sucked all the oxygen out of their bomb shelters. It was an all-round horrific experience, the likes of which had no peer in human history.

which led to wasted efforts and enormous diversions of resources. Hitler and his subordinates feared a repeat of the 1918 revolution almost to the bitter end of the war. They had no way of knowing if the German people would make a sucker out of Douhet or not, and through the war they kept the country's emotional pulse by spying on its citizens. Again, the postwar Strategic Bombing Report concluded:

> The mental reaction of the German people to air attack is significant. Under ruthless Nazi control they showed surprising resistance to the terror and hardships of repeated air attack, to the destruction of their homes and belongings, and to the conditions under which they were reduced to live. Their morale, their belief in ultimate victory or satisfactory compromise, and their confidence in their leaders declined, but they continued to work efficiently as long as the physical means of production remained. The power of a police state over its people cannot be underestimated.

In the early months of the war, Bomber Command's daylight losses proved so severe that the only way to strike at the Reich and sustain an offensive required a switch to nocturnal operations. The loss rate remained appalling, and for much of the war it was higher than the USAAF's. By war's end, 51 percent of Bomber Command's airmen died as a result of combat with the German defenses. Another 9 percent died in accidents back in England, while an additional 3 percent suffered serious injury in those crashes. A full 12 percent of the force ended up in POW camps. Only a tiny fraction—1 percent—bailed out of their flaming bombers and escaped capture. Just 24 percent survived the war unharmed. Those were long odds—worse than those faced by their fathers who served in the trenches at Paschendale or the Somme.

In the years following the war, historians have passed judgment on the British area-bombing campaign and the morality of massacring civilians from the air as deliberate national policy. At times, documentaries or books have stirred the controversy and led to visceral reactions from veterans' groups and those who fought the campaign itself. In the decades to come, as time dilutes the passion and emotions surrounding that era and the last of the wartime generation passes, no doubt new historical perspectives will be offered.

British historian Noble Frankland, himself a veteran of Bomber Command, perhaps best summed up the strategic and moral quandary the British faced during the war in a speech he gave in 1961: "The great immorality open to us in 1940 and 1941 was to lose the war against Hitler's Germany. To have abandoned the only means of direct attack which we had at our disposal would have been a long step in that direction."

Kurt Vonnegut, who had been an infantryman in the Battle of the Bulge and was captured when the Germans destroyed the 106th Infantry Division, presented an opposing view based on his experiences inside Dresden as a POW. After the February raids, the Germans organized the Allied captives in the area into body-retrieval crews and sent them into the devastated city. Of that experience, Vonnegut told the *London Times*:

> It is with some regret that I here besmirch the nobility of our airmen, but, boys, you killed an appalling lot of women and children. The shelter I have described and innumerable others like it were filled with them. We had to exhume their bodies and carry them to mass funeral pyres in the parks, so I know.

The morality debate will continue for as long as historians have an interest in World War II. In light of today's NATO and American policies to minimize civilian casualties, sometimes with such restraint that it risks incurring losses among its own troops, the ruthlessness of the World War II city-busting campaigns seem cold blooded. Then again, the enemy faced—Nazi Germany—was busily sending millions to their deaths in Eastern Europe's concentration camps. And that was just the start of the transformation Hitler and his minions sought to make in what had been vast stretches of the Soviet Union. Not taking any and all measures to stop a genocidal regime would have been a dereliction of moral responsibility. This one moment in history required that humanity be set aside and the gloves be cast off so that the future could be saved.

And what of pinpoint bombing and the American daylight effort? Clearly, had the Germans been left to reorganize their industries for total war and increase production without threat of attack from the air, they could have turned out far more aircraft, tanks and

The vast fleets of bombers created by American factories either were destroyed in place or were brought home to places like Walnut Ridge. Acre after acre of Liberator and Fort blanketed the Arkansas countryside as a testament to the power of a roused United States to meet the challenge of total war.

armaments than they did in the final years of the war. The Eighth and Fifteenth Air Forces destroyed that growth potential and forced the Germans to invest considerable treasure and energy in dispersing their industrial base and sending it underground. This made the Reich's war effort even more vulnerable to the destruction of its rail network, which further hampered production and movement of strategic materials.

When the oil campaign began in earnest in the spring of 1944, that is when Spaatz's command began to have a profound effect on Germany's ability to sustain the war. By the fall fuel shortages plagued every aspect of German military operations. When the Wehrmacht launched the Ardennes offensive in December, the panzers rolled without enough fuel in rear area depots to get them to their objectives around Antwerp. Instead, the Germans counted on capturing large stocks of Allied fuel and oil as they overran the forward most American units. Talk about desperation. The panzer leaders could thank the B-17 and B-24 crews for their nightmarish dilemma. In 1945, the Reich simply ran out of fuel, and the entire nation came apart just as the Allied armies poured across its frontiers.

By sticking with daylight bombing, the USAAF's strategic forces imposed an air campaign on the Luftwaffe that the Germans simply could not win. After their fleeting victory in the fall of 1943, the Germans did not have the resources, pilots or aircraft available to expand its fighter defenses in preparation for the grueling 1944 campaign. When Spaatz made drawing the Luftwaffe into the open a priority in early 1944 and selected targets he knew Goering's pilots would have to defend, the attrition rate soared and the jagdgeschwaders were bled white. In the span of four months, the entire balance in the air over the Third Reich shifted in the Allies favor. This became the single most important pre-condition to the D-Day invasion. Without air superiority over the beaches, the Allies never would have been able to pull off the Normandy landings. Without a doubt, this was the Eighth Air Force's greatest single contribution to the victory in Europe.

The prewar theorists believed that airpower alone could defeat an enemy nation. Armies would become obsolete. Tanks would be so much useless scrap metal, and the infantry-men would be reduced to merely mopping up broken cities in their air force's wake. This singular, almost obsessive vision of modern warfare missed the essential nature of it. Following the 1918 armistice, warfare became the sum of integrated and mutually supporting elements working in concert to defeat an enemy. No single element would be able to do the job alone now as a result of the technologies developed since the start of the century. The modern era of warfare would be defined by combined arms operations.

Douhet, Trenchard, Harris, and to an extent Mitchell, all missed the mark. Eisenhower's Deputy Supreme Commander in 1944, Air Marshall Arthur Tedder probably understood this better than most Allied senior leaders. He believed that the total integration of air, land, and sea operations into one overall strategic framework was the only way to defeat a nation as powerful and dangerous as Nazi Germany. He got it. The strategic bomber was an important component of that combined arms vision, not the be-all and end-all war winner the airpower zealots believed it was.

The skies are empty now, the airmen who fought these desperate and brutal battles above the Europe's burning cities are mostly in their graves. They fought in their nation's defense, steeped in images of freedom and romance that the air seemingly offered. Such naïve visions proved to be a sucker's bet, dispelled completely by the end of their first mission. As the shock of those shattered preconceptions wore off, the men came to realize their futures looked grim and short. They saw men die, saw what flak shrapnel could do to the human body. Some suffered alone in single-set cockpits, their flesh flayed by bullets or shells that sent their mounts spiraling earthward. There were hundreds of ways to die in the air, and those comparative few survivors bore witness to most of them. They returned home with deep scars. The air war cast a shadow across the rest of their lives.

In the decades that followed the war, the vision of what the air war was as told by historians and Hollywood grew more remote from its reality. The vision of the glorious cause in the air crept back into popular culture. New generations found fascinating the aircraft and their technical specifications. Whole publishing industries grew up around this passion, which continues to this day.

Others found glamour in the surviving aces and their tales of courage and daring. At conventions and conferences, they cut rakish and charismatic figures that endeared themselves to countless audiences. They signed autographs. They wrote books. Without realizing it, they contributed to the establishment of a legend that served as a barrier between what people back home wanted to hear and the actual human experience over Europe during the war.

The reality must never be allowed to fade from memory. The aviators went into the war hoping to avoid the pain and trauma of the Western Front. Instead of repeating the attrition in the mud, their vision of a quick way to end war only changed the nature of the carnage. Ultimately, the bloodletting endured longer and claimed a higher percentage of the participants than was experienced in the trenches of World War I. Though the strategic bombing campaign materially contributed to the defeat of Nazi Germany and played a key role in that victory, airpower failed completely in the greatest hope of its prewar advocates: that it could minimize victory's cost.

The airmen paid the price for that miscalculation, but all too often that is forgotten. At its heart, the strategic bombing campaign was a human experience, both to the aviators and to those who suffered under their bombs. Eighth Air Force veteran and poet Randall Jarrell, when seeking a way to convey this to those who never rode into battle aboard a four engine bomber, found powerful words to underscore the humanity sacrificed in the quest for ultimate victory.

> From my mother's sleep I fell into the State,
> And I hunched in its belly till my wet fur froze.
> Six miles from earth, loosed from its dream of life,
> I woke to black flak and the nightmare fighters.
> When I died they washed me out of the turret with a hose.
> —*Randall Jarrell, "Death of a Ball Turret Gunner"*

ACKNOWLEDGMENTS

BOMBS AWAY! WOULD NOT HAVE BEEN FINISHED without the assistance and support of many people. First, a huge thanks to Scott Pearson for his diligence and patience. Hope I haven't caused you too many gray hairs this time around! As always, it has been a real pleasure working with you. Thanks to you and your staff for making me look good, even when I don't deserve it. The talent and dedication at Zenith is truly special, and it is always a pleasure to work with everyone there.

To Richard Kane, I owe a debt of gratitude that cannot be repaid with mere words. Richard ensured I'd have the opportunity to write this book, which has served as an expression for a passion I've retained since my childhood back home in Saratoga, California. Having the opportunity to share some of these amazing photos and tell the story of the strategic air war in Europe represents one of the longest-held dreams I've had, both as a man and as a writer. Thank you, Richard, for helping me realize that goal.

To my family, Ed, Renee, and Jenn. You three continue to suffer through my crazy schedules and long, long days with patience and love, and I would never be able to pursue this difficult career without your support. Renee, you've been a constant source of inspiration for me, and I have loved seeing you bloom as a writer in your own right this summer. Congratulations on your first two published articles, and I cannot wait to see how your skills develop and lead you forward in whatever you choose in the years ahead. Ed, my nine-year-old son, has been able to identify and talk about almost every major aircraft used in World War II since he was able to talk. One memorable summer day when he was barely three, Ed sat in my lap next to my dear friend Bill Runey, who flew P-40s with the 49th Fighter Group during World War II, and successfully named every aircraft in a World War II aviation book. Bill was absolutely astonished. In later years, as Jenn and I ran a photo archival service, Ed would sometimes identify images and aircraft for my bride when I was out on a business trip.

Jenn, you've been my partner and best friend for my entire adult life. Your support and faith in me is what carried me through the dues-paying years. When everyone else gave up, you remained loyal and rock-steady in your support. That means everything to me, and whatever success I will ever achieve will be yours too.

Bob and Laura Archer, your friendship over these past fifteen years has been an integral part in my success as a writer. Thank you for all you've done for my family, and Laura, thanks for your diligence with Vol. You've saved him from Simon's fate, at least for now, and I've treasured the time we get to share together.

Denice, Andy, Brenda, Larissa, and Bob—thank you for making my mornings go smoothly and taking care of me even on days when I'm sullen and grumpy. Shawna Akin, your dedication and support these past twelve years have been vital for me. You keep me organized and sane. Thank you for all you've done for me.

Taylor Marks—your inspiration has guided me this past year. It will continue to do so as I negotiate the road ahead. Not a day goes by without you in my thoughts and prayers. And as time has passed, I've found myself missing you more and more instead of less and less.

Part of this manuscript was finished in the barracks at North Fort Hood, Texas. Among the crickets, the 107-degree heat, and fireflies, I wrote many of the captions in the base's MWR, or on the lower bunk of my rack while embedded with 1-168 Aviation, Oregon and Washington National Guards. I was living with a group of pilots whose dedication to their mission is second to none, one that served as a reminder that the legacy and tradition established during World War II continues to flourish in the ranks of America's combat aviators today. Daryl Jones, whose bunk was next to mine, kept my nose to the grindstone as the clock ticked down to our departure for Afghanistan. Everyone else—Nate, Will, Eric West (thanks for those tips . . .), Brian, Alex, Captains H. and U., Heidi, Craig, Jim—your support and encouragement, as well as your acceptance of me joining you in this difficult journey, means the world to me. Since Emily Shumate pulled me from the flight at Fort Hood August 5, I've focused on finding a way out to you.

These new friends of mine fly CH-47 Chinook heavy lift helicopters. Deployed to Eastern Afghanistan in August 2010, my friends have been split up and sent to FOB Salerno and FOB Shank. On August 28, 2010, Taliban fighters assaulted FOB Salerno while dressed in U.S. Army uniforms. Some wore suicide vests. The men I lived with at Fort Hood, including Daryl Jones, Will, Nate, and Brian, faced the same situation the pilots of the 7th Fighter Command faced on Iwo Jima in the spring of 1945 when Japanese hold-outs launched a banzai charge through their encampment. One Taliban fighter breached the wire and came very close to the 1-168 before he was killed. Thank God none of these incredible Americans were lost in such a desperate and dangerous event.

Lastly, to Allison Serventi Morgan, your work chronicling the U.S. military's relief operations in Pakistan following the catastrophic earthquake there in 2005 is incredibly important and will show your audience a side of America's heart few ever get to see. I expect to see your book on the shelves someday soon. I have no doubt that your talent and drive will bring you rich success in this new path you've chosen. Your assistance on *Heart for the Fight*, *Manhunt*, and *Bombs Away!* has been instrumental and tremendously appreciated. Thank you for your selflessness, for the inspiration you've provided, and the unwavering support you've given me. You are significant. And I'm only saying all this because I want your car (even if it is slower than mine). Or was that last thing too flip?

BIBLIOGRAPHICAL NOTES

Since 1945, few aspects of World War II have attracted more attention than the struggle for Europe's skies. Thousands of books have been published on the subject. A few stand out as pillars of the subject's historiography.

No study of the Eighth Air Force can be undertaken without Roger A. Freeman's body of work. Roger's devoted, detailed, and massive output on the Eighth has set the standard for future generations of historians. *The Mighty Eighth, The Mighty Eighth War Diary, The Mighty Eighth War Manual, The Mighty Eighth in Color,* and *Fighters of the Mighty Eighth* were all indispensible research aids for this book.

Jay A. Stout's *The Men Who Killed the Luftwaffe* (November 2010) offers a fresh and brilliant new look at the USAAF's victory over the German Air Force. This is a book not to be missed. Eric Hammel's *The Road to Big Week* is another excellent account of the 1942–1944 stretch of the strategic bombing campaign.

There are countless memoirs and biographies from veterans of the Eighth Air Force. *Zemke's Wolf Pack,* by Hub Zemke with Roger Freeman, stands out in a crowded field. *Staying Alive* by Carl Fyler is a gem of a book that provides insight into the experience of the bomber crews. Jimmy Doolittle's memoir, *I Could Never Be So Lucky Again,* is an entertaining and useful resource.

To Command the Sky: The Battle for Air Superiority Over Germany, 1942–1944 by Stephen L. MacFarland and Wesley Phillips ranks as one of the best of the new perspectives on the air war. For a more general look at the USAAF and strategic bombing, *The Rise of American Air Power* by Michael S. Sherry is the best single-volume account available.

Since the early 1970s, some terrific accounts of the German experience in the air war have been published. Williamson Murray's *Luftwaffe* ranks as the best general work on the German Air Force. *Six Months to Oblivion* by Werner Girbig provides a detailed look at the Luftwaffe's last stand as it was overwhelmed by the Allies in the final half year of the war. Alfred Price's *The Last Year of the Luftwaffe* is another valuable resource on the subject. *JG-7: The World's First Jet Fighter Unit*

by Manfred Boehme has been one of the most important works to emerge in the past two decades. Boehme debunks many of the myths surrounding the ME-262 and provides ample research to show how those myths developed after the war. For any serious student of the air war, Boehme's book cannot be missed, if for anything than to provide a counter-balance to Adolf Galland's *The First and the Last*. Interesting personal memoirs of men who fought against the bomber streams include *I Fought You From the Skies* by Willi Heilmann.

The RAF side of the air war is well covered, starting with Francis K. Mason's *Battle Over Britain,* a staggeringly detailed book. Derek Dempster and Derek Woods' classic, *The Narrow Margin,* still rates as one of the great works on the Battle of Britain and is a must read. John Terraine's *A Time for Courage* provides an excellent account of the RAF in World War II. Max Hasting's *Bomber Command* remains one of the single best books on the RAF's nocturnal offensive.

Excellent personal accounts of the air war can be found in C. F. Rawnsly and Robert Wright's *Night Fighter*. *Tale of a Guinea Pig* by Geoffrey Page is a particularly poignant account of one member of the Few who stopped the Luftwaffe, at a terrible personal cost.

The books mentioned here represent a fraction of the sources I used for *Bombs Away* and which are available on the subject, but are the ones that I have found most useful or powerful over the years.

Back in 1977, as a nine year old, I found Herbert Molloy Mason Jr.'s *Duel for the Sky* and spent a good portion of that summer floating in my parents' pool reading and re-reading it. It spurred my interest on the European Air War, and I've been collecting books on the subject ever since. This past week, as I moved my office into the old USAF air defense command center's plotting room at Camp Adair, Oregon, I came across my well-worn copy of Mason's book. It now sits on my son's bookshelf in hopes that he will pick it up soon and find a rekindled passion for a subject that has already captivated two generations of Brunings. If it can be found, *Duel for the Sky* is the perfect introduction to World War II in the air for a young reader.

INDEX

★ ★ ★ ★ ★